Also by Michael A. Warnke:

Schemes of Satan
The Satan Seller

Also by Rose Hall Warnke:

The Great Pretender

Recovering From Divorce...

Recovering From Divorce...

There Is Hope and Healing for the Victims

by
Michael A. Warnke
and
Rose Hall Warnke

Victory House, Inc.
Tulsa, Oklahoma
1992

Cover illustration by: Terry Dugan Design
Edited by: Lloyd B. Hildebrand

Publisher's Note

Recovery for the Victims of Divorce

The subtitle of this book — "There Is Hope and Healing for the Victims" — serves to reveal the authors' main theme. There is hope for recovery for *all* the victims of divorce.

Every family, every church, indeed all of society, knows the ravages of divorce. It is decried and denounced from pulpits. The well-known statistic — "one-in-every-two marriages" — is oft repeated. But what is being done for the victims of divorce: the divorced couple, the children, the extended family, the friends, the parents?

This book was written with the victims in mind. Mike and Rose Warnke share their story of struggle and failure in order to bring the taboo of divorce out of the closet. Through their openness about this hidden subject, they offer hope and healing to all who have been victimized by divorce by helping the reader to understand, to grieve, to recover.

If you are a victim of divorce, we pray that *Recovering From Divorce* will meet your deepest needs.

— The Publisher

Dedication

From Mike to Rose

From Rose to Michael

and

*to every hurting soul who
picks up this book . . . .*

Acknowledgments

To our Lord and Savior who showers us with His mercy, grace, and blessings.

To John and Julie Joy, who loved us at our worst.

To Clift Richards, who never stops believing in us.

To Mark Craig for showing us his loyalty and trust.

To Warnke Ministry Staff for their ongoing support. They are second to none, and they make the concert ministry and outreach to those who are hurting . . . . happen!

To Lloyd Hildebrand for his brilliant and insightful editing of this book . . . . his assistance was remarkable.

To our children . . . . Michaelle, Christina, Brendon, Kataryn, Jesse . . . . our grandchildren, Kataryn Rose and Alexandra, for showing us how important it is to strive to become emotionally healthy individuals and to give them the opportunity to grow in themselves . . . . and not in our shadows.

To all those who know us as we really are, not as they expected us to be . . . and still love us.

To John Bradshaw and Thomas Merton and Alice Miller for making such incredible commitments to teach us about our wounded inner child and how to reach and heal those desperate hurting places in our deepest souls.

To Word Records staff for their simple understanding.

And last, but not least, to all our family who give real meaning to the words "loved ones" . . . .

Contents

Introduction   1

Editor's Preface   7

Foreword   15

1. God, It Hurts!   19

2. I'm Scared!   31

3. Hidden Controllers   41

4. Programed for Failure   55

5. Old Pain/New Pain   71

6. Only the Lonely   87

7. What Do I Do With the Anger?   113

8. The Fallen Have a Future   129

9. Mike Warnke — the Preacher vs. the Man   141

10. The Priority of Love — a Lasting Friendship   169

11. Live Your Life as Your Gift to God
     by John Joy   197

Afterword   213

Counseling Guidelines   215

Introduction

The divorce of Mike Warnke and Rose Hall Warnke is not the end of their story — their shared journey through this life. Their divorce is not an ending; rather, it is a transition, a transformation, a new beginning. Pray for them, if you will, in this time of uncertainty. The next phase of their sojourn undoubtedly will be quite challenging. Mike and Rose are entering virtually uncharted relational territory. Pray for them.

Let me tell you about my role in this story. My name is John and I am a therapist who counsels with Mike and Rose. When they first came to me two years ago for counseling, I had never heard of the Warnkes or of Warnke Ministries. At first, all I knew was that I very much liked Mike and Rose. Each is quite creative, outgoing, caring and personable.

However, I also knew from the outset that outside of miraculous, divine intervention, there was no hope for their marriage. The psychological damage for each was too deep and too pervasive from childhood on. Their characterological styles were too fixed; the trust bond of their marriage had been irreparably severed.

Practically speaking, you can't heal wounds as deep and longstanding as theirs are while making your living by performing on the road, trying to keep everything at full production level so that you can provide for your family and continue to pay your staff so that they can provide for their families.

1

I started therapy with Mike and Rose as I traditionally start with couples. I let them know that as their therapist I would follow them down either of the paths before them: the path of marital reconciliation or the path of separation and divorce. I also indicated that I preferred a commitment to at least five sessions to explore their alternatives. I made my bias about the matter quite clear: Follow the path of reconciliation first. Then, if and only if this path proves to be impassable, they should begin to explore the path of separation and divorce. Though I saw little-to-no hope for a successful reconciliation for Mike and Rose, I nevertheless thought it best for them to be open to the possibility of their marriage being restored. They endeavored to be as open as possible to this alternative.

For weeks we worked (counseling with each one individually and with the couple together) in an effort to put the Humpty-Dumpty pieces of their marriage, their lives, hopes, dreams, wants and needs together into a meaningful form. However, it soon became clear that our efforts to reconstruct and resuscitate their marriage were not working. The life support systems had to be withdrawn. In October, 1991, their divorce was finalized.

Yet Sister Rose and Brother Mike and their ministry go on.

It's been a very unusual and enlightening experience for me to work with Mike and Rose. Although I have ferried many couples across that dark river Styx of divorce, I've never done it quite like I am doing with them. Usually after I have ferried a couple across the dark river, the man leaves and moves away, over the trackless terrain, concealing his wounds and secretly blaming everyone available for his miserable fate. The woman, bewildered, lost, and often for the first time on her own, will more often return time and again to the river for therapy. Searching for that something she can never quite find — in me — in anyone. And it's only a very few of these women who remain long enough to learn the secret wisdom of spiritual healing and transformation — the development of a new viewpoint, a new life vision, a new state of being.

Mike and Rose are the first couple I have ever guided together into this territory. Frankly, I wonder if such a process is possible. For this reason, I am asking all of you who are a part of the community of faith to keep us in your prayers. What we are attempting to accomplish here is quite unorthodox. But, of course, what else would you expect of Mike and Rose (and me) but the unorthodox?

The comic artist and the mother-producer are no longer married, but they are joined in their commitment to the ministry. Mr. and Mrs. Michael Warnke have new identities to each other. Instead of being husband and wife, they are now "Brother Mike" and "Sister Rose" (to each other as well as to the community of faith). Their plan is to continue to work and create as partners: artist-to-artist and producer-to-producer. They plan to continue Warnke Ministries together and to do their part to do their best to preserve and reinforce a healthy working relationship with each other, their family and the community of faith they serve.

A noble undertaking indeed.

There was a time when I, as an essentially conservative Christian, thought that such an arrangement would be impossible. At first, therefore, I didn't give Mike and Rose's vision much hope. After all, divorce is divorce. It's horrible, bitter, vile and messy. It's worse in many ways than death itself. The victims of divorce feel abandoned, betrayed, crucified and knifed in the back repeatedly by those they once trusted most.

At one time I felt that "Thou shalt not divorce" should have been the eleventh commandment. Then I was reminded one day of Peter's vision. (See Acts 10.) The Lord told him to rise, kill and eat the unsavory beasts that had descended in his vision. Peter replied, "Not so, Lord. They're common and unclean."

The Lord went on to show Peter what He meant, and the Master's vision was spread to the Gentile world — to you and me. I believe the situation that Mike and Rose face at the present time is a similar challenge. It's hard for us to imagine that there is an oasis of healthy transformation in the wasteland of divorce. Even yet, there are times when I think the idea must be a mirage — a tempting illusion. But then, again and again, the miracle presents itself.

What can you say when you receive such an opportunity from the Lord? One of my favorite notions is that life is like a movie or a drama-in-the-making. I sometimes believe that there are certain scenes we are all eventually called to play. One of these scenes is the humiliation scene. We see an example of this in Luke 7 where a shamed woman comes to the Master in the presence of her critical accusers. What an interesting psychodrama is presented in this passage from the Scriptures.

More and more, I've come to realize that at some time in our lives we are all exposed and we are called to play the shamed one. (Rose and Mike are going through it now, and this book is their alabaster box of ointment. These words are their tears. They are offering their hearts and their story to the Master and to us.)

What will our response be? We may either be their critical accusers or we may act as Christ to them. The choice of the roles is ours: Accuser or Priest. The glory will be the Lord's. Pray that His will be done.

John M. Joy, LCSW, M. Div.
Lexington, Kentucky

Editor's Preface

"We are getting a divorce!" The words stung when Mike and Rose Warnke, my long-time friends, first spoke them to me. As a counselor, I wanted to fix it. As a friend, I tried to deny it. As a minister, I felt so many mixed emotions. As an editor, I wanted to avoid it. As our discussion continued in a hotel room in downtown Tulsa, I soon knew that the stark reality of their imminent divorce could not be fixed, denied or avoided. It had to be faced; it had to be dealt with. It had to be accepted.

As with so many contemporary issues and problems, the Church has had great difficulty accepting the reality of divorce. Many Christians are divorced and many Christians are getting divorced. This book was written by Mike and Rose while they were going through the painful throes of their divorce. It is full of intense emotions but it is also full of hope.

They have allowed themselves to become vulnerable to criticism and negative judgments in order to help all victims of divorce, to let them know that the fallen do have a future and that in Christ there is hope even in the aftermath of divorce. They wrote for another purpose as well: to help believers everywhere to understand the issues surrounding divorce so that they might be enabled to reach out to the scarred, the hurt, the fallen with greater compassion and love.

It is appropriate for all of us to confront the reality of divorce from a Christian perspective. There are times when all of our "shoulds" and "should nots" ring hollow. The horrible pain of a broken marriage, followed by the devastation of divorce, is one of those times.

Like death, divorce involves a process of grief and mourning. Its victims include the husband and wife, the children, the extended family, the friends. When the divorced are involved in ministry, the effects of divorce are even more far-reaching.

In *Restoring the Christian Family,* John and Paula Sandford wrote about the emotional scarring that divorce always causes:

> Divorce is a far greater wounding than death. Divorcees may have the same recurrent sorrows plus all the woundings of rejection. Divorcees often feel ugly and unwanted, undesirable, and they feel they are a burden to others. Particularly wounding both to widows and divorcees is to feel like a fifth wheel among erstwhile comfortable couples' groups.... Today, when divorces are shattering more and more homes, the church needs more than at any other time to rediscover its ministry to singles, divorcees and surviving parents.

(From *Restoring The Christian Family* by John and Paula Sandford. Published by Victory House, Inc.)

As Jesus was called to "bind up the broken-hearted" (see Luke 4:18), so must all of us endeavor to bring healing to the hurts arising out of our human condition.

It is our desire — indeed, our fervent prayer — that God will use this book to bring hope and healing to all the victims of divorce. In many ways, the book is styled as an ongoing counseling session in which Mike and Rose are sharing their fears, feelings, thoughts and experiences very openly. Each chapter is built around a particular topic that relates to their backgrounds, marriage and divorce. At the conclusion of each chapter, I have written a brief reflection on their comments in order to give objective insights from counseling experience and biblical teaching to help clarify some of the issues involved. The concluding chapter of the book was written by the Warnkes' counselor, John M. Joy, who gave them support and counsel through months of turbulence and turmoil. He continues to guide and support them in their admirable journey of recovery.

I first met Mike in the early seventies when I was pastoring in Plainfield, New Jersey. From the very beginning, I knew that this very special guy had been redeemed for some very special purposes in the Body of Christ. When I became an editor with Logos International, I had the privilege of working with Mike once more; his best-selling book, *The Satan Seller*, revealed the story of his past as a satanist high priest and the testimony of his radical conversion to the Lord Jesus Christ.

Through the years, I have come to appreciate Mike's spirit of love and tenderness that is sometimes masked by an aggressive outspokenness, is graced with good humor, and always ministers deeply to the hurting. Faithfully, he has proclaimed God's Word to untold thousands for more than twenty years. He still maintains a rigorous schedule of more than 200 concerts per year!

Early in the eighties, at a Christian Booksellers Convention, I had the honor of meeting Mike's wife, Rose Hall Warnke. Recently married, the young couple beamed with joy and hope. It seemed to be a marriage made in heaven — two very creative individuals united in their deep commitment to the Lord.

Unfortunately, however, they were not prepared for some of the stresses and strains of ministry that came against them. No one, especially Mike and Rose themselves, anticipated that those pressures would break their marital relationship. Like a bridge that is weakened by repeated floods and storms, the marriage of Mike and Rose Warnke was strained to the point of collapse. They sought counseling and the support of friends, but the distance that had grown between them was too wide and too deep to cross.

As you read their story, you will gain new insights into the tragedy of divorce. Many ask, "Why do so many marriages end in divorce?" Christians are asking the same question as it relates to the marriages of believers. Recent studies show that the one-in-every-two-marriages-end-in-divorce statistic applies to Christian marriages too.

When we face this reality we will learn how to be open to finding ways to help couples become better prepared for marriage and how to intervene early on and effectively in marriages that have gotten in trouble. We will be motivated to pray for struggling couples and to come against Satan's attempts to disintegrate the marriages of those who are involved in ministry. We will learn how to attend to and care for hurting people instead of judging them.

The pain of divorce is real. The victims of divorce are real people. Their needs are real and so are their hurts. The compelling honesty of Mike and Rose opens windows of truth regarding this important topic.

These two extraordinary, special people are now in recovery. They've gone through the stages of denial, anger, bargaining, depression and acceptance. They know what it feels like — the pain, the rejection, the anger, the frustration, the doubt, the fear. They also know the hope that is available through faith. All of this brokenness has resulted in Mike and Rose having a greater capacity to understand others. It has drawn them closer to the One who said, "The sacrifices of God are a broken spirit; a broken and contrite heart, O God, you will not despise" (Ps. 51:17).

Rose continues to be involved in a special ministry to abused women in prison. She knows how difficult it is for them to trust another person. She feels the pain they still carry from years of child abuse. She can hear the feelings behind their words. God has blessed her with an exceptional talent in the field of music as well. Her piano playing and her composition of music enable her to reach many people with the love of God. She is also an accomplished poet and, through this book, you will learn how writing poetry has helped her to cope as you read some of her poignant poems.

Mike continues to minister around the world. His books and tapes are reaching thousands of people. One of his videos — "Out of My Mind" — and two of his books — *The Satan Seller* and *Schemes of Satan* — have been enjoying phenomenal sales. All have been maintaining consistent recognition on best-seller charts in recent months. Mike was recently distinguished as the number-one Christian entertainer in Australia.

The ministry of Mike and Rose to the hurting people of the world is best revealed, however, by individual letters from people who have received their ministry. I conclude this preface with an excerpt from one such letter:

> Dear Mr. Warnke: Thank you for ministering to us — my husband and me — during the worst time in both our lives. Nearly four months ago, you were at the high school in our town. Our 8½ month old daughter was at home with her nurse after being released the previous Monday as a hospice patient. She was terminally ill and only lived another 26 hours or so after your concert. Thank you for the two-hour break you gave us from reality . . . I just wanted to let you know how thankful we are to you for picking us up for a few hours and shedding some "Son-shine" on a really black week.

Thank you, Mike and Rose, for your honesty, your love and your vulnerability. May God bless your ministry for many years to come.

Lloyd B. Hildebrand, M.S.
Managing Editor
Victory House, Inc.

Foreword

Brothers, we do not want you to . . . grieve like
the rest of men, who have no hope. . . .
(1 Thess. 4:13)

In the above passage, St. Paul writes to believers
about death and dying. He points out that there can
be hope in grief — a hope that goes beyond death.

Our book has a similar theme, but we are not
writing about physical death. We are dealing with the
grieving process that always follows divorce. Yes,
divorce is a kind of death. Feelings of loss in the
aftermath of divorce are very real indeed, and they are
compounded by a deep sense of personal rejection.
When a marriage fails, self-esteem is shattered in the
same way a hammer breaks a window pane. No
physical injury can possibly compare with the deeply
aching hurts of a heart broken by divorce. We know
these things all too well, because we are now divorced!

Like Paul who was writing to the Thessalonians,
we are writing to believers, particularly those whose
lives have been scarred by the destructiveness of
divorce. People who feel they have nowhere to turn,
no one to talk to, no value to others.

We strongly believe that there is a need for an open
and honest book that addresses the real, nitty-gritty
issues of coping and living and working it out after the
dissolution of a marriage. The victims of divorce do

not have to hide! We are more than statistics! God loves us, and He offers hope and healing to all.

Much of this book was written as we went through the death throes of separation, divorce proceedings and the terror and trauma that is part and parcel of a broken home.

God was there to help us as we faced the fears and turbulent emotions of each new day. Because of our experiences, we are able to write with assurance that we know there is hope for the hurting — for all those who have suffered through a divorce.

We both wish that the reason for this book could have been averted. When we took our marriage vows, the idea of divorce seemed to be a total impossibility. We meant those vows. As time went on, however, our circumstances changed and our marriage relationship strained to the breaking point.

Even as we write this foreword, we can hear the negative judgments and criticisms of those who would like to say, "Well, why didn't you change those circumstances? Why didn't you make it work?"

We didn't know how.

We had lived in denial of our codependency and dysfunctional life style for far too long. The purpose of this book is not to justify our behavior. Neither do we want to blame anyone. We've done enough of that already. Rather, we hope to share our experiences in such a way that we might be able to help others avoid the mistakes we made. We want so much for others to be able to understand the harsh reality of divorce, that it is never something a spouse really wants and that it is painful beyond all description. We want others to understand. Above all, we want people to know that there is hope for all whose lives have been hurt by divorce.

Part of our problem stemmed from our backgrounds. Another factor was our separated time in ministry. We were together less and less as the years went on. Many times, regrettably, we passed each other silently (and briefly), like ships in the night. We failed to read the handwriting on the wall. As the gap between us grew wider, we failed to build bridges.

Yes, we failed. It hurts to admit it, but we allowed all this to happen. It did not just happen to us; it happened because of us.

We know that many will not be able to understand. Some will even hate us. Too many times we hear of believers being rejected by other Christians because of their failures and their divorces. Those who are quick to condemn fail to see the spirit of the law which is love. Instead, they come from a need to control the lives of others. This gives them a sense of power.

The Christian response to any problem that results from the human condition (a state of sin) must always be to reach out to others with the love of Christ, to offer each broken person God's provision of healing and to encourage one another as each of us endeavors to pick up the pieces from our shattered lives.

The words of St. Paul help us to see this need more clearly: "Brothers, if someone is caught in a sin, you who are spiritual should restore him gently. But watch yourself, or you also may be tempted. Carry each other's burdens, and in this way you will fulfill the law of Christ" (Gal. 6:1-2).

In spite of our divorce, we have chosen to remain friends — the best of friends. We remain in ministry together as well. Although we are clearly aware of each other's weaknesses (and strengths), God has given us the grace to continue to love each other — not necessarily *always* to like each other.

Is there hope for the hurting after a divorce? We can affirm that there is. God's grace is always greater than our sin. His love is a deep well from which we can always draw the water of life — if we will receive it.

We are rising from the ashes of our brokenness. We are rebuilding out of the rubble of our divorce. God continues to fulfill His promise:

He has sent me to bind up the brokenhearted, to proclaim freedom for the captives and release for the prisoners, to proclaim the year of the Lord's favor...to comfort all who mourn, and provide for those who grieve in Zion — to bestow on them a crown of beauty instead of ashes, the oil of gladness instead of mourning, and a garment of praise instead of a spirit of despair. (Isa. 61:1-3)

Michael A. Warnke
Rose Hall Warnke
Burgin, Kentucky

1
God, It Hurts!

To hope is to risk frustration. Therefore, make
up your mind to risk frustration.

(Thomas Merton)

Mike:

Somewhere between Santa Fe, New Mexico, and
Tyler, Texas, my breakthrough comes in the cabin of
a small airplane, climbing through the clouds, over the
Sangre De Cristo Mountains. It's snowing down
below, but we are in the sunshine above the storm.
Even so, it is cold.

The world seems so small from up here. Life is
reduced to just this space, and the pressurized air we
breathe. Sunshine and shadow race along 21,000 feet
below and it's time to face myself and a task that scares
the literal hell out of me.

I'm not too sure how this will all come out. The
scratching of my pencil along the page makes my heart
race and my stomach feel funny. It's time for the truth.
It's time to drop the mask. It's time to scrub the grease
paint from my face and put the clown away for a while.

That's not easy. The clown has carried me so long.

Peeking out behind the face
Bringing up a brand-new place
I'm afraid
I've been here before
And it hurts.

How can I do this without seeming to seek self-justification? How do I write about our divorce without seeming full of self-pity? That's not what I want. There is no way to make it right because it simply isn't right. It just is.

The ideal is there before me. I know that it's the best. Falling short of that isn't easy, but that's the way it is.

Is God the God of the ideal or the Lord of what is? Does He live only on the mountain top or is He down here with me? Is it in the achievement of perfection that my salvation lies, or is it the striving even with the failures that make it all real?

I have never been the Christian I should be. I've made more mistakes since I've been saved that I did before I accepted Jesus. Why? Because I've been saved for a longer time than the period of my life before I became a Christian. I spent the first twenty years of my life without the Lord and the last twenty-five years in His service. making mistakes is simply a part of the human condition, isn't it? Just being human. The pitfalls were there and sometimes it seems I've found all of them!

This does not mean that there have not been victories. Nor does it mean that nothing has been accomplished through it all. What has been accomplished, however, has been done in spite of me, not because of me. Even though I've never been the Christian I should be, Jesus has always been the Jesus He promised to be!

Rose:

Divorce is: a relief . . . a death . . . a birth . . . a horrible crime against the soul . . . sorrow . . . pain . . . disorienting . . . destructive . . . heart-breaking . . . grief . . . disabling . . . being lost . . . being alone . . . silence . . . panic . . . hurt . . . anger . . . despair joy . . . fear . . . discouragement . . . distrust . . . paranoia . . . regret . . . confusion . . . opportunity . . . bitterness . . . resentment . . . physical illness . . . awareness . . . being overly sensitive . . . split thinking . . . loss — of your loved one, loss of yourself . . . loss of your personal identity . . . self-pity . . . blaming . . . insecurity . . . hate . . . feeling rejected . . . feeling thrown away . . . feeling violated, neglected, used . . . divorce is a state of shock!

God, it hurts!

First, there is numbness. There seemed to be no reality. What is the truth? Before the torrent of emotions I described above began to cascade over the cliff on the edge of the deep ravine between Mike and me, I felt nothing. It was as if I had been thrown into a deep abyss of darkness. For several months — even years — I was surrounded by nothingness — black, empty nothingness!

As far back as November, 1984, I remember what I would feel when someone would ask, "How do you feel?" or "How are you?"

I wanted to respond (and sometimes I did so) with, "I died somewhere along the way and just don't have the nerve to lie down!"

At the moment of realization that my marriage would end in divorce, "I HAD NO DEFINABLE FEELINGS! Then the maelstrom began. Like a tropical storm swirling into land with dark clouds, destructive winds and monsoon rains, divorce threatened to rip me from my moorings and drown me in doubt and fear!

I will never fully remember, nor fully forget, the moment when I realized my marriage would end. In fact, there have been several moments of realization. The first time I allowed myself to realize it, however, remains indelibly etched in my memory. The deep, searing pain is all too vivid to me even now.

We lived together on a Kentucky farm in the rolling hills near Lexington. Our farmhouse is very old. Most of its rooms have working fireplaces that are necessary to use during the winter months. Beautiful, crackling fires remove the damp chill from the rooms in the cold Kentucky winter.

Early one evening, in December, 1984, I went into Michael's library. The house seemed very cold, so I started a fire. A warm hearth is always so inviting, but on this particular evening I didn't seem to be able to get warm no matter how much wood I threw into the fire. Mike was sitting silently at his desk, and I took a seat on the sofa near the fireplace.

I looked around me. The room was filled with Michael's "treasures." The bookcases overflowed with books on the Civil War, the writings of Arthur Conan Doyle, books by Thomas Merton, autographed copies of Christian books written by our friends around the world, Bibles and teaching books on Christian topics.

Michael has so many gifts that have been presented to him from people everywhere — T-shirts, plaques, cups, pictures, cards and countless other items that he values so deeply. Those precious belongings were in evidence everywhere. His black-powder guns were displayed prominently on the wall above his desk along with many photographs of the children and other family members.

One picture caught my eye that memorable evening — a photo of Michael and me. We were smiling robustly and he had his arm tightly around my shoulder. I remembered how happy I had felt when that picture was taken, and how securely protected I had felt in Michael's arms.

Where were our smiles now? My feeling of security had been replaced by a gripping sense of panic and doom! An impenetrable wall divided us.

On an adjacent wall, I noticed a large watercolor painting. It was the very first gift I gave to Michael. Its blue, hazy colors seemed chilling to me on this particular evening.

What was Michael doing? He always sits at his beautiful, leather-top desk that he loves so much when he is home. Why doesn't he turn around and talk to me? The top of his desk is so very tidy — so tidy that it almost seems empty, cold and clinical. He always has so much to do — no time to stop. In fact, we even made a little joke of it once, "If you want to see Michael, you'll have to go to his library."

I knew we had to talk on this particular evening. We had to talk more seriously, more honestly than we'd ever talked before.

I am so afraid. As Michael turns around, I note that he is very somber. He looks at me with the look a doctor gives when he is about to inform his patient of imminent death. What's wrong? I wanted to know and I didn't want to know. But I had to know.

He sits near the fire in an old, restored, white, wing-backed chair. I am getting colder, so I move onto the floor right in front of the fire.

My heart pounded within my breast. It was breaking even then. "God, I need strength," I silently prayed. I was so scared, but I knew I had to ask.

My words became a knife slicing through the cold and heavy atmosphere of the library. "It's over, isn't it?" I barely managed to squeak the question that broke through all my defenses and my denial. As I said the words, I looked into the fire. I couldn't bear to look at Michael. I didn't want to see his eyes when he told me what I didn't want to hear!

My peripheral vision enabled me to see him sitting with his hands together in his lap, his legs crossed, leaning back in the chair. He almost seemed to be tucked into that big white chair. The cold quietness that followed my question threatened to smother me. After several minutes passed, Michael leaned forward in his chair. He was ready to give his answer. I wanted to put my hands over my ears like a frightened little girl who did not want to listen to any more criticism. The silence was broken by Michael's soft voice, "It's not your fault. You have to know that. It is not your fault."*

The softness of his voice betrayed the harshness of his message. Those words. Those awful-sounding, final words! I hate those words! Their finality echoed like the vibrations from a gong, and my head began to throb.

Tears streamed from my eyes. Then I screamed, I yelled. Fear gripped me further as I was transformed from my "let's talk" mood into my yelling, screaming, don't-tell-me-anything mode.

As usual, we both began to follow with all the blaming, shaming and verbally abusive comments you can think up when you are hurting and feel so devastated by this kind of emotional pain. An emotional pain that feels like you have fallen into a black hole in outer space! I was drowning. . . .

The fire died down and went out while the inferno of our emotions raged. As the fire died out, so did my heart.

*Note: For five years after this, we tried to make it work. Life became an emotional roller-coaster ride. Actual separation, however, did not occur until 1989.

Lord, how long will this continue to hurt?

The writing of poetry was therapeutic for me. Indeed, writing this book has been too. I encourage you to keep a journal of your feelings and experiences, to try your hand at writing poetry.

So many insights come to us when we write our thoughts and feelings. Simply expressing them on paper results in a new measure of freedom.

I wrote the following two poems in 1991 prior to our divorce. I hope reading them ministers to you like writing them ministered to me.

> *Looking Back*
> *We were sharing.*
> *Time*
> *And life*
> *And tender things*
>   *As best we knew----*
>
> *We were children*
> *Sharing our toys*
> *Just walking along*
> *Glad to be together*
> *Both of us wearing blinders*
> *And never really thinking*
> *About the roles we'd have*
> *In each other's life*
>
> *I don't know when*
> *I felt like running*
> *Or why he chose*
> *To let go of my hand.*

I only know
We walked together
And now I walk alone.

(Rose Hall Warnke)

Michael

The years took part of him from me.
Some of him fell off of me
        Naturally-----like leaves

In time,
Some of him will turn into other names.
And later,
To another gray hair against my face.

I'll lose a lot
But just the same,
I know I'll keep
Parts of him-----
        Parts of him.

(Rose Hall Warnke)

Editor:

The two short lines of dialogue that Mike and Rose spoke in the library of their farmhouse reveal so much about some of the dynamics involved in divorce.

Meekly, Rose asked, "It's over, isn't it?"

She didn't want to ask the question; she didn't want to hear the answer. One suspects she knew the answer already.

That's the way it usually is when a marriage gets in trouble. Both partners, and everyone else, try to go on with life as if nothing is wrong.

In counseling and recovery circles, this phenomenon is known as DENIAL. In a sense, it is the same thing as believing, "If I ignore the problem long enough, maybe it will go away."

Most often, denial involves a lot of wishing, pretending and hoping. Sometimes it leads to bargaining (with God and others). Such negotiating might take the following form: "Dear God, please let it not be true. I'll do anything if you will only let (my husband/my wife) stay with me."

Note the sense of panic that pervades this prayer. A child-like quality of begging also enters the picture. The hurt, inner child cries for acceptance and help.

At this stage, the frightened partners of a failing marriage begin to withdraw. They isolate themselves from their partners, family members and friends and retreat into themselves.

Such hiding behavior is symbolic of their need to retreat from conflict and confrontation. This is usually seen in adult children of alcoholics and survivors of abuse. (Both Mike and Rose were victims of child abuse in various forms.)

The breakdown of interpersonal communication is a clear sign that a marriage has entered troubled waters. If any of these symptoms regularly occur in your marriage, it is time to seek the help of a counselor. (A minister should be able to put you in touch with a competent professional.)

The lack of communication and the child-like dependency that Mike and Rose had been experiencing in their relationship led to a dysfunctional (not working) family relationship. This is known as codependency — a situation in which two people become attached in such an unhealthy manner that they drain each other of all energy to invest in the relationship. This results in each partner becoming an enabler who allows the other to get worse in his or her areas of weakness instead of helping him or her to get better.

Oftentimes, a wife or a husband will find this preferable to the dissolution of a marriage or separation because of the security issues involved.

It is important to notice how Mike responded to Rose's question. He said: "Just remember — it's not your fault." If we actively listen for the feelings implicit in that statement, we become aware of the guilt that he was feeling at the time. He felt guilty for being away so much, not attending to Rose's needs, and for making her feel so hurt and all alone.

This reaction is not uncommon. Mike was willing to assume all the guilt for what had happened in their marriage because of his own set of hurts and his personal brokenness. Such guilt is a burden almost too heavy to bear, and it needs to be resolved through intensive counseling and prayer.

When a marriage is in trouble, the focus should not be on blame-shifting, but on ways to resolve the crisis. Most marital problems have a multiple causation involving both partners. If recognized and dealt with early enough, such problems do not have to be insurmountable.

Feeling guilty and being hard on yourself usually do not add to the resolution of the problem; such feelings are likely to compound it.

This is one of the messages that is inherent in this book: *seek help for your marriage early*. It is reported that more than 80% of troubled marriages can be saved if outside intervention occurs early enough.

Regrettably, for Mike and Rose it came too late. The problems had festered too long. Neither of them had any energy left to invest in their marriage. When they began to step out of their denial, it was already over.

2

I'm Scared!

Give to the winds thy fears;
Hope, and be undismayed;
God hears thy sighs and counts
    thy tears;
God shall lift up thy head.
    (John Wesley)

Mike:

I wish I could stand in front of the world and proclaim, "Be like me. Follow my example." Many people would like to hear that from me and others. I'm not the only one who can't seem to grab onto perfection. Most everyone is stumbling along somehow. It may not seem so when we look at some people, but that's just because some folks are better at doing life than others. Not as many mistakes, or as big, when they do come. But everyone is dealing with something, and our choice is to face it or to fake it.

When people can't be perfect themselves, they look for a surrogate — the pastor, the prophet, the evangelist, the teacher, the athlete, the entertainer, the politician, etc. And because of their shortcomings, they expect more from their substitutes than they do from themselves. And we try to live up to that expectation, those of us who have been chosen as role models.

Do you know how scary that is? When others expect us to be perfect, and we know all too well how empty and un-healed we are on the inside? It's terrifying! But reality comes calling. We have to face ourselves. We need to get honest with God, ourselves and others. That's really one thing that's wrong with the Church today — we're not honest with one another, ourselves and God. We wear our masks to church and we play church, pretending all the time that everything is okay instead of saying openly, "Look at the mess I've made."

Being human and making mistakes are facts of life — real life, that is. When I realized that Rose and I would be getting divorced, I knew that it was time for us to put our fantasies to rest. We were not the perfect, model couple we had wanted to be. Our farm in central Kentucky was not Camelot. The plain, ordinary truth was that we were two broken people who were drawing on each other's weaknesses and enabling each other to get worse instead of better. We were (and are) a man and a woman; we never were the demi-gods that others seemed to think we were (or that we tried to be).

It's scary to be this open. I feel very vulnerable. Some will want to crucify us for our failures, I'm sure of that. Some of those we love and serve will want to cut us off. The fear of contagion is so great that it is better in many people's minds to kill the surrogate instead of taking the risk of failing by association. This kind of thinking goes something like this, "I put my trust in him or her and he or she turned out to be just like me. If I had wanted that, I would have trusted myself in the first place."

Oftentimes not living up to expectations is regarded as heresy. And heretics get burned at the stake! The smell of smoke is what keeps a lot of us in hiding!

Many times I have preached that the only way to go honestly to God and before mankind is to do so as yourself. To put aside the mask, and take to God and mankind the person you really are with no holds barred and no strings attached. One needs to be careful of what he preaches because 100 times out of 100 you'll get to live up to what comes out of your mouth!

That time is here for me now. Not that I haven't tried to do this all along. I've so often been so much myself that I've chased some well-meaning people away in my ministry, my public life and my challenge to the status-quo. But now it comes down to me — ME. Not the clown, not the commentator, not the critic, not the satirist — but ME. Naked, little *me!*

I'm at the point now where I am forced to lay down my dreams, my fears, my sickness, my shortcomings and my failures. Frankly, I'm scared. Truly scared!

Rose:

How is it that we can know when a death is approaching? How is it that we can feel so intently when we know we are losing the person who is sitting right next to us and they haven't even left the room?

How is it that when your mind, your soul, can no longer endure any more emotional pain, it begins to go numb, become blank, and all about you loses its color, its taste, its feelings, its sound, and all that's left is nothing? It is a feeling of *no* feeling!

That fateful December night in Michael's library that I described in the preceding chapter was one of the most frightening experiences of my life. The room began to grow dim even though the lights were still on. Simultaneously, my life began to grow dim even though I was still breathing and my eyes were open. I began to feel pathetically small, totally insignificant. I felt as though I was dying or perhaps I already was dead.

I remembered my study of some of the modern poets who wrote about death-in-life themes. T. S. Eliot's "The Waste Land" and "Hollow Men," for examples, and Allen Ginsberg's "Howl!" My life had become a "waste land," I felt hollow and I wanted to howl at the top of my lungs! I was hopeless.

Hopelessness! It is a place where death occurs!

As I look back now, I know it was only my love of God and my children and my belief in their love for me that gave me the will to live. Little did anyone around me realize what was happening to me. Hiding myself! This became my ultimate goal. I was even hiding from myself!

Divorce! What an ugly word! What an evil villain! There isn't any adequate way to describe it. There are no effective words to help someone understand it. There are no feelings that truly reveal it. There is only DIVORCE! Stark, frightening DIVORCE!

Why me? Why divorce? Why? I had to find some answers. In my earlier book, *The Great Pretender,* I had written a poem that reveals some of my earliest steps toward self-discovery:

> *I'm so tired---*
> *Tired of what?*
>
> *Tired of the darkness*
> *The darkness of love*
> *Weary of me, yes, me.*
>
> *Fragmented, scattered,*
> *Torn from myself that*
> *I was — to the me I am*
> *Who am I?*
>
> *Pretending to be what*
> *I'm not you see*
> *Pretending to be what*
> *I'd like to be.*
>
> *Free from this world*
> *That kills the free*
> *Rid of those who*
> *Consume---*
>
> *Tearing my heart and*
> *Soul at will*
> *Can they be stopped?*
> *From destroying me?*
> *The me I want to be----*

This ugly monster called DIVORCE! has entered my life and caused me to come face to face with who I really am. That's a scary business. Divorce — the reality — therefore, is both a death and a new opportunity. It is a great teacher and a counselor. It has taught me that I am not and cannot be perfect in myself. I am a human being — nothing more and nothing less. This is not an excuse for my mistakes because I realize my perfection is in the Lord Jesus Christ.

As a result of certain experiences in my childhood, I entered adulthood with a deep-seated, driven need to perform. One of my problems has been that I have wanted, striven for and cried out for my own perfection. I believed it was attainable! After I became a Christian, I even wanted to believe that because of my faith I could become immune from mistakes, immune from sin. Perfect! After all, many who were role models of Christianity for me seemed to be perfect. Surely I could be too!

How quickly we begin to learn to stand when we begin to realize we have fallen down. How much sweeter life is when we realize how bitter it can be. How much quieter we become when we realize the necessity to be still. How much greater peace we will have when we tire of the battle to be the only one who is — Right!

The temptation was (and is) so great to try and justify myself, to explain, to excuse, to blame, to deny responsibility to uphold my innocence, to defray responsibility, to fill my mind and heart with insignificant junk. I have gone through the "if only's," the "what if's," the "I should haves," "I could haves," "he should haves," "he could haves," "they should haves," etc. Yet, as time passes and healing begins to come, these temptations become easier to overcome, even though they don't go away.

I don't like divorce. I never did. I don't even agree with it! I cannot understand fully how two people who begin loving each other end leaving each other. I realize it isn't the best thing to do, but I know now that there are times when it becomes the only thing to do.

I am a survivor — a survivor of this devastating thing called divorce! I've seen it crush the weak, kill the strongest, consume the most caring, disable clear minds, divide, and destroy. It is a living hell! It is like a head–on collision that takes place at seventy miles per hour with your whole family riding on the hood of the automobile. It is a death (that you think will never end) with no funeral and no burial.

For some, it is even an escape attempt. Certainly, it is not an end. Divorce does not end the problems of the individual spouse who is affected by it. Sometimes, but not always, it ends the problems that existed in a marriage. Often, however, it creates even more problems.

As I face the future, I'm scared but I'm also hopeful. My faith in Jesus Christ helps me to face my fears. A poem that Christina Rosetti wrote in the middle 1800s describes my outlook·

> I have no wit, no words, no tears;
>   My heart within me like a stone
> Is numbed too much for hopes or fears;
>   Look right, look left, I dwell alone;

I lift mine eyes, but dimmed with grief
    No everlasting hills I see;
My life is in the falling leaf:
    O Jesus, quicken me.

My life is like a faded leaf,
    My harvest dwindled to a husk;
Truly my life is void and brief
    And tedious in the barren dusk;
My life is like a frozen thing,
    No bud nor greenness can I see:
Yet rise it shall — the sap of Spring;
    O Jesus rise in me.

My life is like a broken bowl,
    A broken bowl that cannot hold
One drop of water for my soul
    Or cordial in the searching cold;
Cast in the fire the perished thing,
    Melt and remould it, till it be
A royal cup for him my King:
    O Jesus, drink of me.

Editor:

The title of the chapter, "I'm Scared!," reveals the terrifying fear that victims of a troubled marriage and a divorce must come to grips with. It is an intense fear that colors every aspect of life. It is a fear of failure, a fear of the future, a fear of one's self, a fear of insecurity, a fear of what people will think, a fear of self-disclosure, and a bag full of several other fears. When these are grouped together, the result is terror!

These fears may keep a person from seeking help. As Rose pointed out, fear may lead a partner in a marriage to attempt to justify his or her actions.

How does one deal with fear — a fear so intense that it is like the fear of dying? First, he or she must recognize the source of the fear(s). In Mike's section, he dealt with the fear of self-disclosure by recognizing that hiding the unpleasant truth of their divorce would not help anyone. Both he and Rose are bravely taking the risk of sharing information that they know will cause others to evaluate them negatively.

It is very important to get over the hurdle of caring what others think. A person who is motivated by what others think is coming from a performance orientation that was learned in childhood. Rose alludes to this in her section by discussing her perceived need to always perform perfectly for others in order to be accepted by them.

Ultimately, each of us has to be able to live with ourselves. We need to be true to our convictions and values even when others find them unacceptable. When we are Christians, this becomes easier because the strength of Jesus is made perfect in our weaknesses.

Both Mike and Rose are discovering that the place of ultimate security and acceptance is found in the lap of their heavenly Father. He has become their safe place. When one is secure in Him, there is little room left for fear. But this gem of security takes work and commitment for it is not as easy to find as it sounds.

Such emotions are normal, however. Bringing them into the light of God's love takes away their power and control over us. Jesus said, "Then you will know the truth, and the truth will set you free" (John 8:32).

As Rose pointed out, the feeling of hopelessness brings death. The antidote for this poison is love. God loves you! He does not want you to be hopeless. He has an answer for you. "There is no fear in love. But perfect love drives out fear. . . . We love because he first loved us" (1 John 4:18, 19).

Go to God honestly with your feelings. He wants to listen. He will hear the cries of your heart and He will be your very present help.

3
Hidden Controllers

I was a stricken deer, that left the herd
Long since. With many an arrow deep infixt
My panting side was charged, when I
    withdrew
To seek a tranquil death in distant shades.
There was I found by One who had himself
Been hurt by th'archers. In his side he bore,
And in his hands and feet, the cruel scars.
With gentle force soliciting the darts,
He drew them forth, and healed, and bade
    me live.

(William Cowper, 1731-1800)

Mike:

Hurtful memories, though long hidden, have a great influence on our attitudes, behavior and feelings. Both Rose and I brought sacks full of such painful memories into our marriage. These unresolved hidden hurts controlled many of our responses to one another.

I vividly remember a time when I climbed into my father's lap. He had been drinking. As I settled down for a snuggle, my father reached down beside his chair and brought up a beer bottle and smashed it in my face!

"Son," he said, "there's only one thing I can really teach you. Never trust anybody!" That happened when I was six years old.

I never could really trust anyone to just love me. I've always tried to secure the love of another by doing what I thought would cultivate it.

Early on, I learned that if I did what was expected of me I would win approval from others. What I didn't understand was that this kind of approval is not permanent. "You can't buy love" is an old cliché; nonetheless, I have found that it is true.

Basically, I was a good little boy. My folks were both heavy drinkers, and how they treated me sort of depended on the level of alcohol in their systems. One moment they could be loving and kind, the next they would turn cruel and brutal. There were hugs and there were beatings. I never knew which to expect. I tried to do the right thing so that the love would stay and the hurting would stop. Sometimes it worked. Usually it did not.

My mother was never quite as tough as my dad, but she died when I was eight years old. She was killed instantly in an automobile accident. She had been drinking. Somehow in my child's mind I thought she had left me because I hadn't done enough to keep her with me. This suspicion propelled me to try harder with my dad.

Three years later, my father also died. A ruptured aorta caused him to bleed to death. The night he died, I was home alone with him. I was the one who held him as he slowly passed away. He was bleeding from his nose, mouth and rectum. The bed and both of us were covered in blood. They found us in the morning and rushed him away. He died about three hours later on the operating table. Nothing I could do had made him stay. Alcohol was the main cause of his death, but I thought it was my fault somehow.

Following the demise of my parents, I lived with aunts. Eventually, I moved in with my half-sister and her family. Again, I was sure that if I did just right I would be loved and accepted. Those were the necessary prerequisites to my being loved. The cruelty had stopped. Finally, I was treated well and with love. There was just one thing that troubled me in the home of my sister — every time I "messed up" I was told that if I didn't do right I would be sent away. There's no way I can explain how the fear of that punishment hung over me. It was always "try harder," "prove yourself," "be perfect." Could I ever be *good enough?*

Later on in life, after I became a Christian and went into the ministry, my sister and her husband did not approve of my choices for reasons that I am sure were very valid to them. They have not spoken to me in the last twenty-five years!

I continued to try and I continued to fail. I gave what I had to the people in my life but somehow my ability to be real about love had been damaged. Instead of loving the way that's healthy, I continued to try to buy acceptance and favor instead of giving *myself* —

a capacity I did not understand and it frightened me. I gave things or actions that were geared to bring me a return. When the returns stopped coming, I ran. And the others ran too.

One of the most horrifying things that can happen to a person is to live in a house full of people who "are no longer there." Their bodies may take up space, but they are far away. Hollow eyes instead of expected smiles. Talking about everything and saying nothing at all. Flashes of something real that might have been at the first, but always returning to the distance and the emptiness.

Rose:

As Michael and I searched for the deeply hidden memories that could give clues to our present problems, I decided to seek professional counseling. I found a wonderful Christian counselor, John Joy, in Lexington, Kentucky. With John's support and guidance I was able to plumb the depths of my despair and find some answers. In order to get ready to face the future, I had to take a look at my background. For me, as for Michael, the good memories were mingled with the bad.

My mother — oh, yes, my mother. I am now able to accept her, to love her more fully, to understand her more — her losses and her pains.

I have learned that although she had been harshly punitive at times and always very controlling, the way she had been treated in the past was how she treated me. The power of her tongue, her tone of voice, her way of looking at me caused me to fear her. She was so busy being a mother, she sometimes forgot to love me.

Constantly, repeatedly, she taught me the necessity for always being correct and proper in everything I did and said. She permitted me to wear only dresses or skirts with blouses or sweaters — but preferably dresses. I can still hear her saying, "Rose Mary, put your skirt down and keep your hands in your lap." "Now, keep your legs together and sit up straight." "Hold those shoulders back when you walk."

Later, when I was around ten years old, I was allowed to wear some blue jeans. My mother always felt that jeans were for working people from poor families.

It was a very empty way of life! Always being told how to act, what to wear, how to sit and stand, what to say. Literally, I was unable to think for myself.

My Mother

In me
You carved yourself———
All of your fears
Your doubts
Your guilts
Your loneliness

You carved in me
An inequitable mixture
Of weakness
Of strengths

Of motives
Of love

Your memory is so different
Than mine
They are both fantasies
They are both real

And will I seed the lives
Of my own children————
As you did mine?

You lived in search
Of one more chance
And I was another opportunity——
I can not be that chance
I can only become who I am———

Once I found a shell,
So small and battered
Nestled in some sand
Humble and rough
And honest
Like you.

I never cared what you looked like,
Only what you felt like
You were my mother
I knew you even when I was blind————

(Rose Hall Warnke)

My father was seldom at home, at least that I can remember, because of the demands of his business. He spent most of his time working.

I attended a very exclusive private school in Kentucky. Known as a "finishing school," I'm sure my mother must have felt that this school would continue the training she wanted me to have.

In my new school, I learned about manners, social appearances, and I received a thorough training in the arts and foreign languages. After school hours, I was tutored in French several evenings per week. I was twelve years old at the time.

My French teacher was a matronly woman who had her hair pulled back tightly in a bun. Sometimes I wondered if she was so grouchy because her hair bun was too tight!

Another of my teachers, a Mrs. Charm, had a sadistic twist in her personality. Once I saw some small, dark objects in her hand and I assumed they were licorice candies. "Mrs. Charm," I asked, "what is that you have in your hand?"

She was well aware of my interest in candies, so she replied, "Oh, these? Would you like some?"

I couldn't thank her fast enough. Never, ever will I forget those "pieces of candy." With eagerness, I threw a handful of those round black pieces into my mouth. No sooner did I do so, however, and my mouth began to draw shut. Unbeknownst to me, I had just begun chewing on an entire mouthful of the most nauseating black coffee beans ever known to civilized man! I choked and gagged while my classmates guffawed. I couldn't spit the residue from my mouth because "spitting is never acceptable." So there I sat! Mrs. Charm, in all her glory, grinned proudly and said,

"Now, class, let this be a lesson to you. Things are not always what they seem to be. Isn't that right, Rose Mary?"

To this day, the smell of coffee gives me a queasy feeling.

In addition to the academic studies, there were ballet classes, tap dance classes, piano lessons, singing lessons, social tea lessons — and on and on!

It was quite a curriculum for a young lady who wanted only to climb trees and play basketball, football and baseball, to ride horses and to be held in someone's lap and to be loved for her self not just for what she did.

No matter what I did (for my mother and some of my teachers), it never seemed to be enough.

I learned and learned and learned. I learned to dance, to sing, and I learned how to serve tea properly. I even learned how to walk with a cup and saucer on my head and not drop it! But most of all, what I learned was that I was not good enough!

Through all that learning I sank deeper and deeper into a well of loneliness. Each day my heart broke with comments like, "Now, Rose Mary, I know you can do better than this." "What in this world do you mean, you don't like to go to dance classes? All the other girls like it."

Little did anyone seem to know or care how I felt. Always being compared with others was a typical manipulation that was used to get me to conform. Through this technique, I also learned to make comparisons. I compared myself with all the tiny, trim girls in dancing class. I felt that I really stood out, with my fat legs and rotund stomach. If I ever expressed my feelings about my appearance, the response would always come back, "Why, Rose Mary, you aren't fat; you're just pleasingly plump and healthy." "Those other girls are so skinny that they look awful. I bet their mothers don't ever feed them good home cookin'."

It was around this same time that I asked to be allowed to take piano lessons rather than dancing. At least with piano, I didn't have to stretch those tight hose over my fat legs and stand up in front of everyone whom I felt were staring at me.

Mother's favorite comment when I wanted to start something new was, "Yes, I know you love piano, but you probably won't finish it any better than anything else you have started!"

Little did she know how much piano meant to me — or how much music would become a part of my life! What a best friend the piano would become to me.

Then there was the constant issue of clothes. More comparisons: "Of course you know you can't wear jeans. Only tomboys wear clothes like that. For heaven's sake, when are you going to learn how to act right?"

After twelve came those horrifying years of becoming a young woman. Boys, parties, dating, high school — to me, it was a time of one humiliation after another.

Not being able to date until I became sixteen was not uncommon for a school girl in the fifties. Being ahead of my age somewhat in school years made the age rule even more difficult. I was a junior in high school at age fifteen and sixteen. Most of the people I knew either had boy friends or had been allowed to go places with their friends since the beginning of the junior year.

These restrictions might not have been so difficult if they were not rooted in a particular irrational fear that my mother expressed to me on several occasions. My mother was terrified that I might become pregnant!

One particular moment stood out during these difficult times of growing up. It centered around the fact that I hadn't started my period yet. By this time I was nearly fourteen and a half. Mother decided I needed to have a physical, so off to a woman doctor we went. Discussing female matters was taboo.

I was amazed by her concern, and blurted out, "What makes you think I am pregnant?"

"Well, you're nearly fifteen years old and you haven't started your period."

This was followed by her long explanation about her fears of my becoming pregnant out of wedlock. She feared I would become pregnant by an unacceptable person (someone who was not from our social status), and then my life would be ruined.

In fact, *her* life might be ruined, and *her* life would be over, etc. "Young lady, under no circumstances are you going to be allowed to bring shame or disgrace or condemnation upon this family!"

As it turned out, my problem was not pregnancy but female problems that might eventually cause me some trouble with having children. What a shock to mother! I could have told her I was not pregnant, but she would not have listened to me. I always felt that my opinions didn't count to mother or to anyone else!

Now I am able to look back on all of this with clearer understanding. I am learning to understand my mother better, and I am realizing that she was doing the best that she knew how to do. Sometimes understanding enables one to forgive easier.

I share these incidents from my past with one goal in mind: to help others to understand why Michael and I were so hindered in our attempts to build a lasting marriage. I trust that greater understanding will enable many to forgive us. I also hope that the understanding of our circumstances and backgrounds will help others to understand their particular problems in order to find help and healing.

Editor:

Both Rose and Mike experienced various forms of abuse while they were growing up. This left them scarred in many ways. Both learned to feel that they had to be perfect in order to be accepted by others. Both felt guilty about normal human emotions. In fact, both had a hard time knowing what was normal, acceptable behavior.

When two people from dysfunctional backgrounds enter into a marriage relationship, it is predictable that they will experience serious problems in their marriage unless they seek help.

Mike's dad taught him not to trust anyone. As a result, I'm sure Mike had a hard time trusting Rose. Rose was taught that she wasn't good enough, that she would never finish anything. It isn't hard to imagine what that "taped message" within her brain did to her view of marriage.

In addition, Mike is an adult child of alcoholic parents. In recent years, we've discovered the long-lasting effects of growing up in an alcoholic home: a general feeling of uneasiness, a need to feel responsible for the choices of loved ones, an inability to confront, a pretending that there are no problems, a deep-seated insecurity, suppressing normal emotions, etc.

Basically, both Mike and Rose felt that they could never be good enough. Neither one felt loved for who they were. Consequently, it was difficult for them to love and accept themselves and each other.

These "hidden controllers" in your life can be identified. When they are recognized for what they really are — emotional programing that comes from critical parents — we are able to face them. Despite what others may have done to us, it becomes our individual responsibility to change our attitudes, feelings and responses. You do not have to be controlled by hidden, unknown forces. Through counseling, prayer and openness you can learn what those forces are and deal with them.

As with all sins and imperfections in our lives, we need to learn to take them to the One who is perfect. He makes all things new. He loves you with an everlasting love. He is a Father who can bridge the gap between the love you actually received as a child and the love you should have received.

As we give Him our brokenness and strife, He is able to take the pieces of our lives and transform them into something beautiful. There is hope for the hurting.

With the willingness to work at unveiling your hurting self to those who can help you, and a commitment to that work, there is healing for you.

Sometimes your tears will help. Feel your emotions honestly. Don't stuff them down deep inside as victims of abuse and children in alcoholic homes frequently do.

Dr. Joyce Brothers, a well-known psychologist and author, lost her husband to death two years ago. She has learned how to survive and to deal with her grief. She said, "You need to be good to yourself. It's not a tribute to the person you have lost to make your life smaller or to not have joy in your life. Crying gets stress out of the system. There is no timetable for grief, but little by little, joy comes back in your life."

Be gentle with yourself. Yes, you've made mistakes. But it's not all your fault. God loves you, accepts you, forgives you. Now it's your turn to do the same.

4

Programed for Failure!

When the conflicting currents of the
unconscious create engulfing whirlpools, the
waters can again be guided into a single current
if the dam sluice be opened into the channel
of prayer — and if that channel has been dug
deep enough.

(Dag Hammarskjold)

Rose:

It has been said that many of us have "taped"
messages recorded in our brains that play over and over
again: "Try harder." "Please me." "Hurry up." "Be
perfect." "Don't cry." "Be strong." Other messages from
"critical parent" figures may play over and over again
as well. Let's talk more about my mother.

My mother and I are good friends now. Her
perfectionism programed an unforgettable message into
my subconscious. As I've gotten to know my mother
better, I realize that many of her "speeches" to me were
coming from her own past and her sense of personal
inadequacy.

How well I remember the first time she "sat me
down" to explain to me how things were. I was five
years old. I had gone to a friend's house after school

to play. My mother came bursting into my friend's house, enraged about my being there and pulled me out of the house.

When we got home, she made me sit in a big, winged-back chair for the rest of the afternoon. I vividly recall how I fell asleep while my mother raged on and on, "What right do you have to just up and go to somebody's house without being given permission? What makes you think you can do anything you well please? You'll learn one of these days, young lady! Wait till your father gets home and hears about this!"

From that point on, I heard the same message countless times. Many of these commandments and slaps of guilt continue to echo in my mind:

"What will the neighbors think?"

"Who do you think you are?"

"You are a disgrace to the family!"

"I will not permit you to bring shame upon this family!"

"What is the matter with you?"

The family image — her image — was more important than my life, my mind, my heart. It was of paramount importance that we be invited to the right homes, go to the right country clubs, attend the right parties. We had to dress properly at all times.

Obviously, these values that my mother held so dearly were main items on the agenda for becoming somebody. But who? Who was it that I was supposed to become?

Most of my childhood memories until age seven are vague if not altogether blank. Some of the more vivid recollections are, regrettably, the more painful ones. One thing I know for sure is that my growing up was very difficult — a turbulent time of confusing thoughts and conflicting emotions.

We spend a lifetime trying to discover who we are. Establishing our unique, independent identities is an elusive process. Trial and error followed by error after error lead us to greater self-understanding. Sometimes I think the Pennsylvania Dutch are right when they say, "We grow too soon old and too late schmart!"

I am quite certain that all of us have painful memories — remembrances of mistakes we've made, unjustices we've received. How do we turn these memories from stumbling blocks into steppingstones?

They are tough schools for learning about life, but it is through such experiences that we gain greater self-discovery. We learn something about personal responsibility and clear thinking when we dare to confront the truth.

Who am I? Where am I going? What is the meaning of life? I realize that I still struggle with these all-important issues. Every time I felt I had succeeded in latching onto some answers, I ended up feeling disappointed and confused.

As a child, I thought I was ugly, fat, unloved and unlovable. My thinking went something like, "Of course they don't love me. How could they?" One thing I knew for sure, I didn't like myself. You may be able to empathize with how I felt. Many of us suffer from feelings of low self-esteem.

I thought I was making some progress toward self-discovery in my teen-age years. I knew what some of my key interests were. At that time, I was attracted to a high school basketball player who was a very nice, tall young man. He was not perfect, however. In some ways, I even felt sorry for him.

He called me one evening and asked if he could come over to pick me up and take me to the game. Predictably, my mother said, "Absolutely not!" You see, this young man's family lived in a part of town where only the very poor resided. His clothes were worn out and his teeth needed to be straightened. All of these features translated to "Disgrace!" in my mother's way of thinking.

Finally and reluctantly, my mother agreed to take me to the game. She underscored the fact that she would be staying there with me! This was mother's usual tactic — to attend an event with me and then to give me a full report later on concerning what I should or should not have done or said.

(By citing my mother's messages and methods I am trying to show how certain attitudes became ingrained in me. These attitudes led to problems in my marriage. Those problems were *not* my mother's fault; they were results of experiences and attitudes that I developed in response to life experiences.)

As I watched the game, occasionally I would catch a glimpse of my mother watching me from across the gymnasium. She didn't look very happy, and I had come to the conclusion that she looked unhappy most of the time because of *me!*

Mother, needless to say, spoiled an otherwise fun evening. On the way home, she lectured me again. In the car there was a long period of silence (the calm before the storm) that was followed by a harangue: "Well, just what is it you think you are doing with trash and no-good people like that?" She then proceeded to tell me what kind of person I was and how I was embarrassing the family. Next, she launched into her usual dissertation about boys — how they were only interested in "one thing," and so forth. Of course, mother never would say what that "one thing" was!

When we got home, my mother ordered me to bed! Actually, I was glad to receive that commandment. Unfortunately, however, she quickly followed with, "I'll be up in a minute to finish this!"

At this point, it didn't seem as if life was worth living. The pain I felt was greater than my ability to reason it out. Why was I always wrong? Why did I cause such unhappiness for others? The only thing I wanted was to stop the pain I felt and to get rid of the incessant litany of my faults that mother seemed to love to sing.

Learning to deal with depression is hard for people of any age. When you are a teenager, there seems to be no hope because coping skills are often deficient at this stage.

She didn't want to hear my answers. There was no discussion. Mother appeared interested only in blaming, scolding, striking out, accusing, humiliating and destroying my sense of self-worth. Little did I realize that her own lack of self-worth was woven into every word and tone. Truly, SHE WAS LASHING OUT AGAINST HERSELF!

As I got ready for bed that evening, I kept thinking, "Life just isn't worth all this! I don't want it anymore!" Many suicides stem from these kinds of feelings. The suicidal person wants to kill the pain the hopelessness, the fear.

It was a time of confusion, chaos and hopelessness. My mind sought a way to escape. I remembered the bottles of medication in the medicine cabinet. "Maybe if I take all the pills, I will go to sleep for good," I reasoned.

Suicide! It wasn't the first time I had considered this "solution," nor would it be the last. My helplessness was attempting to kill my hopelessness. I didn't want to be rid of myself; I wanted to be rid of the pain.

Yes, I know the importance of being a good example. I am very familiar with the expectations to do good, be good, think good, and by all means to stand strong against all odds. But to know is a far different thing than to do.

Even as I write this, I hope someday I will get over this feeling of pleasing others versus being true to myself. Yes, I hope. . . I pray. . . that the day will come when not even a flicker of a moment will swell back up in me those awful memories of feeling like I am nothing, that I have no one.

My walk with Jesus over the past seventeen years has been truly incredible. Though I was programed for failure, He has reprogrammed me to realize that His love for me is unconditional. It is not based on how well I perform. Nor is it given only if I do everything right. He has given me salvation, physical and emotional healing, comfort, safety, security, promise, power, forgiveness, grace, understanding, truth, ministry and most importantly, a Friend who is with me always. I know He understands.

In a way, I'm thankful that I've experienced these kinds of failures because it's in my failures that I can recognize and appreciate my successes. I recognize my need for Jesus. Through His love, there isn't anything I can't do or become! And profoundly I know, without Him I can do nothing of any lasting value.

My Soul

There are places
Within me
No one could ever know.
At the bottom of myself---somewhere
Broken, empty faces
And dreams I nourished
Since I was wide-eyed
And five
And wanting to believe in everything.

Tears can't always fall from eyes,
And some things are just too deep
Or quiet
To be talked about,
Maybe only thought about
When I'm alone
On a beach

Or looking out
Across an ocean.

If you love me
Let me go
To those places within myself
Where I can never take you-----yet,
And where
You must never ask to go----still, let me
Know you will go-----if I want you to!

I heard one minister say, "Why do we worry about success? We're failures to begin with!" At first, I wondered why he said that. Now I think I understand. It's kind of like what St. Paul said in Romans 3:23: "For all have sinned and fall short of the glory of God."

In our failures we see our need for God. He loves you and He wants good things for you!

Mike:

Though I too was programed for failure, there were many victories along the way, both great and small. It was all God. He led me and He supplied my needs.

Recently, I told a friend about this project — a book about our divorce. I explained that it would not be a book on how to avoid divorce, but rather a book to show what happens when it happens. It is not a book about who to blame, but a a book on how to live. My friend, like myself, was frightened to death.

"I'm not sure the public is ready for that," he said. My friend was worried about my career. He's a good friend.

Maybe he's right. Perhaps no one is ready for this book. Could being "up front" about our failure cost it all? That's the chance I must take. Rose feels the same way. We both have come to the place where we know that the only real choice we have is to go on *as ourselves.*

I will not try to speak for Rose. She is more than able to do that for herself. Neither will I try to justify myself, because truly there can be no justification. Wrong is wrong. What has happened has been wrong.

I will not try to say that divorce is a good thing. I can say only that it does happen. That it's real.

In the face of that reality, however, I am able to paint a picture of the grace of God. He is the Master of the valleys as well as the mountain tops. In my weakness, He is made strong.

As I've already stated, I'm scared. Knowing that He loves me is my source of peace.

When Rose and I first got together, I was a very warped person emotionally. I saw in her the chance for love and family I had never known (or if I did know, I had let it slip through my fingers because I didn't know what real love was). Rose lived in the mountains, far away from the record business, far away from "the road." She represented a safe haven in the storm. With love and kids and a home. To me, it was like I had stumbled into a story too good to be true. And it was.

At first, things went very well. Falling in love is the fantasy. Life is real work. As things with the ministry grew, we had to move out of the mountains to be closer to an airport. At the time, I'm not sure either Rose or I quite understood what leaving the mountains would mean.

We bought an old Victorian house in Versailles, Kentucky, a small town close to Lexington and the airport. About the same time, we took over the ministry. Rose had our old cinder-block garage converted into an office. We were running the business in our back yard! As the ministry grew, it spread into the house and into our lives.

I remember one particular morning as I was sleeping late on one of the rare occasions when I was home and had the opportunity to do so. I was awakened by the feeling of someone standing over me. I opened my eyes to find my secretary waiting there with papers that needed my signature. It was total madness!

The more that stress entered our lives, the more the distance between Rose and me grew. The more she threw herself into the work, the less time we had for our life together. The more we were separated, the more our separate lives developed. The more this happened, the greater my fear of rejection and loss became.

I began to fall into my old pattern of providing rather than giving. Trying to buy the love and affection that I saw being turned into energy directed toward work. Rose wanted more and tried to tell me, but I didn't understand. I tried to give what I didn't know how to give and wound up doing only what I did know. More providing, more things, and staying away from the pain. Needless to say, we were arguing all the time. As the volume increased, so did the distance between us.

This is not to say that there were not flashes of effort. There were times when we really tried. Afterwards, we always returned to the same old scenario. Our relationship dwindled and our partnership grew.

We didn't know how to change. Rose had her own problems to deal with. "Demons" of her own. Things from her past were triggered by my actions and vice-versa. All of this added to the unpleasant stew of our marriage. We were both emotionally dysfunctional, and all our old hurts and fears drove us more and more into our own worlds and farther and farther apart.

Lots of new hurts happened during those years as well. I tried in the only way I knew and it didn't work. Rose did what she could, and was never able to reach my fears and resentments. We both offered what we had and none of it was what we really needed. We learned to fend for ourselves. We became two people with only one bond — the ministry.

In spite of all this, the Lord continued to use us. Rose wrote some of her best music during this time. She also wrote her book, *The Great Pretender,* and did a lot of concerts with me. The Lord had provided us with help. The best kind of people. This enabled Rose to create more and to be in the office less. We should have been able to use the extra time together to work on our problems, but by now we were so into the way things were that leaving our own separate lives for one together was beyond our ability.

Work! Travel! Concerts! Records! Tours! Night after night — smiling and laughing, preaching and praying. People were blessed, saved, and lives were changed. God was using us in spite of all our problems, because no matter what, we kept right on doing our jobs. The problems continued to mount, but we were determined to do what God had called us to do.

So many times, situations can cause people to turn their backs on the Lord. No matter what was going on, we couldn't bring ourselves to say no to the people God had asked us to give ourselves to.

It wasn't God's fault. We had carried a lot of unresolved trash into our relationship. We were the ones who were emotionally crippled. And even though our personal relationship seemed out of our grasp, we were and are able to function in the arena where God placed us. I'm not sure how to explain it. I just know that it is.

Some people believe that if all is not well, God cannot be served. We have proven that this is not true. Through it all, we never once gave anyone less than our best. The train of thought these days seems to be that perfection is the only sign of God's blessing. I too believe in the the resurrection power of God. I also realize that Jesus had to be crucified before He was resurrected. God needs to be God in the bad times or

He has no right to be God in the good times. And He has every right!

There will be those who will turn their backs on us because of the mistakes we've made. Those who feel we are no longer worthy to tell of the love of God. But we are, and the Lord knows it. All through the Bible and church history, God has used imperfect men and women to do His work. Holy people, not because their lives were without problems, but because their hearts belonged to Him!

> Nothing can happen in the world save what God wills. He does all, arranges all, makes all to be as it is. He counts the hairs of our head, the leaves of every tree, the sand on the seashore, the drops of water from the mighty ocean. . . . What seems to us weightiest is as nothing in the eyes of God. . . . The real way to get relief is to give one's self up heartily to God; to accept suffering because God sends it to purify us and make us worthier of Him.
>
> (Fenelon)

Editor:

Marriage and parenting are two situations in which most people eventually find themselves. Very few people, however, receive formal training in either area. It seems as if society assumes that it will all naturally fall into place somehow.

When problems occur in either the role of parent or spouse, fear and depression frequently result. Part of the fear is the fear of failure. The depression usually stems from feelings of shattered self-esteem which both Rose and Mike experienced.

The emotions that often lead one into a state of depression are fear and anger. Fear of failure, fear of the future, fear of rejection. Anger at oneself, one's circumstances, one's sense of inadequacy. When these emotions are turned inward, the result is always depression.

Fortunately, for both Mike and Rose, these negative experiences and feelings led them to seek help in God. Through faith in Him they were able to get through the crises while retaining a measure of hope.

God is "a very present help in time of trouble" (Ps. 46:1). He loves you and wants to help you.

No matter what your circumstances, it is possible for you to turn to Him. He knows how you feel; He hears your cry.

> God is our refuge and strength, an ever present help in trouble. Therefore we will not fear, though the earth give way and the mountains fall into the heart of the sea, though its waters roar and foam and the mountains quake with their surging. There is a river whose streams make glad the city of God, the holy place

where the Most High dwells...Be still and know that I am God.

In most cases, our parents always wanted us to succeed. But along the way, they made their mistakes as well. Perhaps they tried too hard, said the wrong things, gave us poor examples to follow. Those things do leave their scars. Like Mike and Rose, we feel that somehow we've been "programed for failure."

There is healing for those scars, and hope for the future. With God's help, recovery is yours! Begin to reprogram your life with professional help and the Word of God.

5

Old Pain/New Pain

I believe that problems can be dissolved by
grace, like a mist is dissipated by the
sunshine... In the climate of faith, a life that
has seemed to be nothing but a tangle of
problems looks quite different. The problems
disappear without anyone actually solving
them. This process of dissolution is all the
more definite if one does not try to find
human solutions, but relies rather upon God's
grace....

(Dr. Paul Tournier)

Rose:

As I write this chapter it is springtime. I am
looking out the window of my farmhouse. There are
two wonderful ponds below the hill in front. Four large
white ducks and nearly 200 wild Canadian geese are
gliding across the water. I counted them earlier this
week — it was a calm way to spend time. For miles
around me I can see rolling hills carpeted with fresh
green grass, bordered by black plank fences. There are
a few cattle grazing in meadows here and there. The
trees are bare. Soon the leaves will come — soon!

I am no longer in shock, no longer completely numb. The destructive, negative feelings that devastated me for so long every day, twenty-four hours a day, resurface only periodically.

As the birds sing so gently and the wind stirs in the big pine tree near my window, I begin to sense the music of hope rising in my heart. Soon the buttercups will emerge from the sod and burst into a yellow symphony along the fence. Although it is cloudy this morning, as I write, I know the warmth of the sun will come again.

I will never be able to forget the awful days, but from now on I will be able to remember them with a spirit of grace, a heart of peace, a clearer mind. In some ways, it seems as if I am able to see things more clearly now than I ever was able to even in childhood when all of my days were filled with anger and fear and rejection and loneliness and nothingness and hate and...and...and....

Again and again, throughout life, if we do not gain a grasp on our hurts...if we do not recognize how dark and how deep those places of pain are, and we do not begin to champion them to recovery and healing, they contaminate the present with as much force and destruction as if they were happening for the first time in the very present moment!

How can I allow my old pains to contaminate my present moments once I become aware of the 'old pain" source? This is the hard work of the soul. To be able to live in the NOW while still being dictated to and even sometimes controlled by the past. And even while knowing this, to claw your way through those horrible memories that make today feel as dangerous and hopeless as thirty years ago!

Yes, even to write it causes me still to feel the old pain. But I have to remember it is *old* pain. And I must not forget or allow it to become *now* pain any longer.

To better explain how and why these pains work like they do I can give an example (from just last week). It was Wednesday around 4:30 PM. I had started to teach a class at the Kentucky State Women's Prison in Pee Wee Valley, Kentucky. It is a class on Abuse and Recovery. As I was speaking to the sixteen women who attended, I began to notice one of the women staring (actually, glaring) at me. She is a tall, slender woman who is around twenty-seven years old. She wears glasses that have a dark tint in the lenses. Her name is Vernita.

She sat back in her chair, somewhat slumped, with her arms folded across her chest. Her hair was parted down the middle and it laid in several chopped straight lengths down to her shoulder. Vernita's head was down and cocked a little to the side. Her dark eyes glared upward at me. Both her feet were on the floor.

As I continued to talk, her staring became harder and harder. That hard, cold look — where had I seen that kind of facial expression before? It began to make me feel so helpless. And the longer I noticed her staring, the more helpless and fearful I became.

Finally it hit me! It was the same look my mother used to give me — that hard, cold look of disapproval.

I turned to this young woman and said, "Vernita, the way you are looking at me is reminding me (or triggering within me) some of the old pains in my life. I know you have no idea that this is happening to me and I also know that what you may mean by the way you are looking at me is probably very far from what it means to me. But right now, I am not going to allow myself to begin to feel bad over an old pain!

"This is exactly what I am talking about with you gals today. I was an emotionally abused child — just as most of you were, whether physically or emotionally, or both. (Any abuse is ultimately emotional.)

"We must never allow those old pains, those old familiar looks, those old destructive attitudes, those old familiar tones of speaking, those old ways of feeling and hearing to contaminate our lives any more.

"We are not children any longer. We are grown women with our own abilities, our own minds, and with the help and love of Jesus Christ as our Savior and best friend, we can remake our entire childhoods and begin a victorious recovery!"

This is what each of us can do to become whole once again — we can begin to recover from the old pains of the past. I thank God that I am in recovery. He is healing me. Though I couldn't trust many people in the past (especially myself), I now know I can trust Jesus, and I am learning to begin to trust myself.

I Only Meant To Love Him

I (we) learned to forgive
We tried to say it out loud
But the words
Hit upon our faces
Like small stones.

Feelings, unedited, denied,
Ran underground in us.
Our eyes became transparent
And I became afraid.
The terror of maybe not
Being together anymore
Became its own justification.

I did not mean to contaminate
His life
With my own confusion,
To allow his need for me
To encourage the collective myths
Little girls are fed for breakfast
I did not unite with him
So that he must divide himself.

> *I only meant to love him*
> *I did not mean to come this far.*

I believed in Cinderella.
I even looked for magic dragons
In my own yard.
I grew up believing. He grew up trying not to.
And I've lived long enough to know
As much as I had been deformed by fantasy,
> *He had been mutilated by reality.*

We are learning to translate our silences now.
We know what it means; sometime.
Feelings that I (we) kept sealed
And beyond each other's reach
Are threatening.
But are becoming defined and honest.
I don't know yet
What parts I'll play in his next life,
But I've come a long way
Trying to find out.

Together or alone
The decisions are beginnings
Like noise———————
My being was formed by others
Before I knew who I was
Now my experience is a prism
Through which I see everything
Differently now.

Differently enough to escape the pollution
Of public opinion against the
Cultivation of "Forever"?
Do I have enough respect and trust
In myself?
And in you?
Do I have enough life
To make the exchange
Enough love to pay for what must be?

I only meant to love him
I did not mean to come this far.

(Rose Hall Warnke)

Mike:

For about three years I carried a small .22 calibre pistol loaded with hollow points in my suitcase. Every morning upon awakening, I took my pistol out of my bag, laid it on the desk or table in my hotel room and took out a sheet of paper. I would then divide the sheet into two columns. On the left, I listed all my reasons to die. On the right, my reasons to live. I had a deal with myself: as long as the list on the right side was longer than the one on the left, I would face another day. But if the morning ever came when the balance would swing the other way, that would be the day when I would "pack it in"!

I don't carry my little revolver any more. The right-hand list was always the longer one. My blessings always seemed to outweigh my trials.

That fact in itself didn't make me feel better, however. It didn't take my pain away. All it did was to keep me alive.

It is so embarrassing to face our humanity. And so lonely, especially when you feel you have no one to go to.

The Christian ministry business (I mean that just the way I wrote it!) is a very, very strange place in which to find yourself.

Ministry is a call from God. Blessed are the men and women who are called to do it. But there is a side to it that can be very sinister.

When I first came to Nashville, at the beginning of my recording career, I thought that everyone who claimed Christ was a Christian. I believed that Christians conducted business in a Christ-like manner and that all was done to the glory of God. It didn't take too long to find out that I was greatly mistaken. What a blow that realization was to me!

I'll never forget the time when I was asked to take part in a large awards ceremony attended by a great many Christian artists. It was my first time to be involved in that capacity. I was very nervous. To proclaim Christ and practice comedy in front of strangers is one thing; to do the same before your friends and peers is quite another.

I stood before the crowd and delivered what I thought was a funny, challenging talk. The meat of the message was about being real. Not putting on what you don't have. Not to just do things to get a reaction and forget to put out the Word. You can imagine how I felt when I was greeted with cat calls and booing. I left the stage only inches from tears.

Later that night I asked a good friend of mine, a man I respect, what I had done wrong. His answer was simple, "You made the mistake of thinking that this was a spiritual gathering. You tried to make a spiritual point, and this is only business."

Over the years I have learned this lesson time and time again. The competition in the business is intense. Record contracts, management deals, and numbers are the things that motivate many to do anything to get ahead. It can all be very depressing for someone who doesn't want to play the game.

About ten years ago, the Lord instructed me to change the rules of how I play. This did not find favor with many of my contemporaries, but that did not matter to me. I knew I had heard the Lord, and that was that.

Part of His message to me was: *no booking agent and no more entertainment at the expense of the ministry!* I knew that I could still be entertaining, but I had to always remember that the message had to come first.

The one person who caught the vision, who believed in what God had said to me, who put herself behind it 100 percent was — Rose!

Surprisingly, however, that was the beginning of what eventually became a major wedge in our relationship. Had I missed God? Had we spun off in a direction that couldn't be blessed? Not at all.

There are times when bad things happen to good people for the best of reasons. It's important to keep things in their proper perspective and to keep our priorities in order. Zealousness can be one of the best ways to bend things out of proportion.

We threw ourselves head-long into the pursuit of the ministry God had given to us. I spent most of my time "on the road," while Rose usually remained at home, managing operations, bookings, etc.

As the years sped by, business became my reason to live. Every minute of almost every day was taken up with work. Rose and I had little-to-no personal life. I was gone all the time. I saw Rose little and was at home less. And when I was at home, I had nothing left for anyone. Because I usually was not at home, the running of the house and family, as well as the operation of the ministry, fell to Rose. As a result, she was forced to come up with a system that couldn't depend on me.

When I did come home, and tried to be a father and a husband, I found that those things were not needed — that *I* was not needed! Actually, I caused more trouble than I did good! I resented this a lot. I didn't realize that consistency is part of the parent-spouse picture, and that wandering in once in a while to trumpet like a bull is not enough.

One of the key factors in a relationship is stability. Stability builds a sense of security and when security is lacking, the strong individual will take steps to stabilize on his or her own. He or she will learn to survive without the help of a counterpart, and one will wind up on the inside, while the other will be left out.

I was out. It was my own fault. But not knowing this, I succeeded in convincing myself that the calling was all that mattered, and I was just unappreciated and misunderstood. The seeds of bitterness had been sown. I felt rejected. I was working myself to death and getting no personal support. That is how I saw the scene.

And the demands on my time just continued to grow. More and more speaking requests, more and more time away, and more and more a business run by two individuals rather than a marriage of two people becoming one flesh.

It was awful. But who could I go to? Whom could I trust? Many people in the business seemed to think that destroying another ministry made what they were doing seem more viable.

Gossip was (and is) a rampant scourge. To show weakness was to invite disaster. You never knew who would talk. Who might blow the whistle. What you might say in confidence could wind up in some Christian gossip column.

Once while in Florida, for example, a "friend" of mine who is a pastor asked me how I was. And because he was a "friend," I told him. "My ass is dragging," I said. (That's what I said.) Then I went on, "My heart is broken. I am losing my grip." In the concert later that night in his church, I didn't have an altar call. Still later, to make matters worse, when I returned to my room, I watched a pay movie on television.

About two weeks later, I received a letter from my "friend" that stated I was no longer welcome in his church and no longer spiritual enough to preach from his pulpit! Why?

He outlined the reasons:

1. I had cursed. (I had used the word "ass.")

2. My life was not in order!

3. I hadn't done an alter call, and that's what he had expected.

4. I was watching pornography in my hotel room! (The actual movie was "Running Scared.")

Not only did he believe all this himself (which was certainly his right to be sure, even if he didn't take time to ask how he could help or offer to pray with me!), but he also took the time to offer his views to everyone he could reach by phone. That was four or five years ago and I'm still suffering from the slander. My "friend" is gone. He's no longer at the church. But the tale remains.

I know of another Christian artist who went to her pastor with personal concerns regarding her own marriage and shared her soul with this man in confidence. The next day she entered the bookstore in her church and found that her own pastor had ordered that all of her records and tapes be removed from the shelves as unfit for Christian consumption!

There were people I could trust. There are people I can trust. I could have gone to them for help, but I was so ashamed. I had failed at marriage before, and I couldn't bring myself to ask for help this time. Besides, at the time, I wouldn't have known what to ask for. I could have criticized Rose, and complained that I was not getting the personal support I needed at home, but would that really have been true? In a way, I suppose it was, but that was just a symptom of the real problem. And even if I had been told, I'm not sure I would have listened.

I prayed for a miracle. I prayed that God would show Rose the error of *her* way. I prayed that God would take my responsibility for me, and that I would not be made to face the facts and dance to the music.

I stayed gone. More and more, I felt separated from my peers and alienated from my wife. I was alone in my own mind. The ministry grew. More and more people were blessed. God blessed the people in the seats, and I continued to wrestle with my personal "demons." Rose continued to learn to rely on herself. And one day I realized what had happened: I had a business partner and not a wife! I had made it happen and I didn't even know I had!

If you convince yourself a thing is true, if you conduct yourself as if it is, when it finally comes true, you are so far into it that there is no going back. To learn too late may be the hardest lesson of all.

During all this time, no one really knew. Some suspected, but no one really knew. To hide the pain, I was funny and I kept busy. Night after night I smiled and laughed and preached. Sometimes, before I went on stage, I had to vomit in my dressing room to settle my stomach, and still, no one really knew.

Rose and I had build a ministry, and we were determined not to let our personal problems become an excuse for giving up what God had told us to do.

Editor:

Emotional pain, either old or new, is one way our minds and hearts tell us we need recovery. As Rose so vividly described, sometimes new pains trigger memories of old pains. When this happens, we need to feel the emotion that has been unleashed, we need to face it and we need to distinguish the old from the new.

Your past cannot be changed. It can, however, be accepted. When we come to grips with the realities of the past and present, we are better enabled to find our way to recovery and peace.

The Serenity Prayer helps us to see this more clearly:

God, grant me the serenity to accept the
    things I cannot change,
The courage to change the things I can,
And the wisdom to know the difference.

When we recognize the source of our pain as being a past experience that we cannot change, we are better able to cope with it. Since we are able to change our responses to past and present pain, we need to put our focus in that direction: learning how to identify our pain and changing our way of dealing with it.

In a marriage, we cannot change our spouse. Ultimately, we come to understand that the only person we can change is ourselves: the way we respond to others, the way we deal with circumstances, the way we cope.

Regarding feelings, we soon learn that denying them or trying to suppress them won't work. Those feelings are there to guide you to seek help. They are real and the way to find healing for their pain is to seek the support of someone who can help you.

For so long, Mike and Rose felt that they had no one to turn to. They lived in a world of anxiety and pain. Mike's vivid description of his denial helps us to see that not dealing with old and new pain can even lead to physical symptoms.

Feeling so alone and hopeless, both of them contemplated suicide. They were seeking a release from their pain. Finally, the pain became so intense and severe that Rose first, then Mike, went to Dr. John for counseling. He listened, he reflected their feelings, he gave advice, and new insights were imparted to both of them. Through greater openness and honesty, the healing process had begun.

There is help available to you that will enable you to cope with your emotional pain. It takes courage to seek that help. You don't have to go through the suffering alone.

Open your heart to someone who can help.

6
Only the Lonely

No man is an island, entire of itself; every man
is a piece of the continent, a part of the main.
(John Donne)

Rose:

Divorce is the result of being unable (or unwilling)
to have an adult relationship. It sometimes comes as
the result of never having been allowed to be children
in childhood. Some children are never permitted to feel,
to experience, to enjoy simple, easy moments of
unhappiness or happiness that fill the process of
growing up. Childhood was a lonely time for me.

Alone with my feelings. Feeling lonely. Scared.
Sensitive. That's how it was and that's how it came to
be again — in my marriage. I can still hear the harshness of my mother's words: "Rose Mary, straighten up
right now! Stop that crying or I'll give you something
to cry about!" Another familiar message reverberates
in my mind: "Rose Mary, settle down! You are too
loud. Nobody wants to hear your loud, screaming
voice!"

In my child's mind, I translated these messages
into: "You are a terrible person! No one likes you!"
Loneliness! Worthlessness!

This was part of the excess baggage I brought into my marriage. I had never learned how to be a grown-up. How to feel good about myself. How to accept myself and feel my feelings. I was never allowed to make decisions or to develop confidence in myself.

When I was sixteen, my father experienced a series of nervous breakdowns. From that point on, he was hospitalized off and on for three years. My mother and sister left my father and me to care for each other during this time. Daddy was very ill, and I felt so helpless and inadequate to deal with his condition. I felt rejected and alone.

Finally, a friend's father helped my father get some permanent help. For six months dad was hospitalized and this treatment was followed by outpatient care for another six months. During this time, I was left completely alone except for the friends who helped with my dad. Being left so alone at that age, under those circumstances, became nearly unbearable for me. I felt totally abandoned — by my mother, my sister, my family and even by my father! It was devastating.

An emotional illness is oftentimes harder to deal with than a physical illness. My mother did not seem to be able to deal with my father's problems. She engaged in denial, believing that it wasn't true.

I knew something was seriously wrong with daddy. When I would visit him in his hospital room, he would just lie there and stare at the ceiling. He didn't seem to know what was taking place around him.

Once when I was visiting he said, "I'm going home." He walked to the nurses' station and said the same thing. The nurse simply replied, "That's nice," and went on about her business. Daddy just went back to his room.

It was so scary to watch him in such a state of confusion. As I said good-bye and left him that evening, I began to cry, possibly more for myself than for him. I got out to the parking lot and turned around to look up at the window of his room. I could see him standing there, looking out. I felt like I was leaving him in prison. I began to sob. Daddy placed his hand on the window as if to say good-bye.

After a few months my father was discharged from the hospital. He came home to a cold house in January. Our housekeeper was gone. I was doing the cleaning, the cooking and the laundry. There were working fireplaces in the house; if they weren't in use, there would have been no heat.

My father hadn't recovered. He tried to kill himself several times. I became his rescuer — a role I was pleased to assume for him.

"Daddy"

Wade, you will never know me.
We didn't have time, or know how————
I would have liked to have known you
And given you something of me.
I wish you could know how I loved you
Looked for you in faces I've passed on the street
   Looked for you in pictures and names
    The looking sometime became the challenge

I looked for you in other men----

I thought I could find you
In things you kept with you
  Two gold pens — now worn thin
  A Bible with underlines that you read
  A house you even wanted to live in
  In people that said they knew you
  In a corduroy coat you wore----
    You wouldn't believe how many hours
      and in
    How many hands I have looked----
  Time covers us all with changes----changes

Katharyn is more funny like you, that I
  remember
Michaelle is more gentle like you, that I
  remember
Christina is more exact like you, that I
  remember
    I am probably more like you, than I
      remember
    People say we look alike---you were
      very handsome

I find now, that the only way
  To find you---is
    To find myself —

I will look for me now.

                              (Rose Hall Warnke)

Divorce is the result of children who never learned
how to receive or give healthy love. I was never

given a healthy love that said, "Life is a celebration and an adventure, and you are created to be worthy of that celebration!" Often I was told, "You just wait until you are on your own, young lady, then you'll see how hard life really is."

Life! It seemed so threatening. Adulthood, so menacing! The world, so scary! Was nothing predictable? Was the road of life meant to be paved by pain and suffering?

Divorce is the result of children who never learned how to trust. I was never shown that I could trust others and that they could be depended on to be there when you needed someone!

I was never allowed to feel that I could be trusted either. Repeatedly, my mother would say to me, "The problem here is that nobody can tell you anything; you think you know it all! Well, let me tell you, little girl, you don't know anything!"

Loneliness! Aloneness! Despair! Rejection! Pain!

Divorce is the result of children who never learned they deserve respect or appreciation, who never felt they were valuable. I was not respected as a child. Neither was Michael. I was not appreciated. Neither was Michael. We felt we had no value. How often this feeling was reinforced, "Don't speak unless you are spoken to. Children are to be seen and not heard!"

How can I expect my child or children to grow up emotionally healthy, to get married, have more children, and have a stable adult life with emotionally healthy relationships when I myself had a very unstable childhood that made me emotionally unprepared for adult life!?

I am convinced that we, as an entire race of people, are as primitive emotionally as if we were still living in caves! Most of us become spouses and parents and yet very few of us ever receive any training in either area except through the role models we observe when we are growing up!

There is very little hope (for those of us who come through the horrors of any abusive-type existence) to be properly prepared and to succeed in adult life and adult relationships unless...unless....

We can first realize...accept...become educated emotionally...and begin to deal with all the hurts, the anger, the hatred, the complete annihilation of self we've experienced.

We must first embrace ourselves before we can embrace one another.

I must first grieve my losses, grieve my days that can never be again...for me and for those who are no longer. Grieve for them — and let them go!

Then and only then, can I begin to celebrate my life, and ultimately to celebrate yours with you.

Yes, the old pain is enormous. When it is added to new pain, it is devastating.

Do I cry or hurt or feel remorse or grieve? Yes — yes — yes!!!

This is the part now that begins the healing — not just the healing of having gone through a divorce or going through a divorce or being in a divorce, but a

complete healing! A healing of forty-seven years! I AM
IN RECOVERY!

Are there others like me? Yes, there are many.
Perhaps you are one of them!

We do not have to live our lives alone. No matter
how alone we feel. Everything we feel, everything we
do, everything we think, everything we say, everything
we are influences someone else — influences all those
around us and influences and creates a world in which
we all live.

Few of us ever realize the enormous responsibility
of ourselves to ourselves or to each other.

I am a valuable, worthwhile person. you are a
valuable, worthwhile person. WE DESERVE THE
LOVE OF OURSELVES AND EACH OTHER!!!

> Yes, I do at times feel lonely.
> Terribly lonely. Yet somehow
> I know that out of loneliness,
> if you can face it, and if you
> can renounce self-pity, and if
> you can overcome the great urge to
> blame other people, then there can come
> a strange but wonderful experience of
> being alone. . . . I still need Him. I
> don't know why this should be. It is
> the way God the Creator made us. To
> go into aloneness without Jesus could
> drive a person mad and even to suicide.
> Don't seek aloneness unless you enter
> that with Him. He could take it, you

can't. I have known people who have
gone into loneliness and on into aloneness without Him, and as far as this life
is concerned, 'they' have ceased to exist,
even though their bodies have stayed alive.

However, with Him, it is in aloneness
that the real treasures lie. You will
find Him in a way that otherwise you
would not. You will love in a way that
otherwise you could not. You will find
what it is to be a real human being. I
have only started the journey but I know
the path, and I know that following it
is what being alive is all about.

(Roy Trevivian — *So You're Lonely*)

Thirteen Years
(6/8/75 to 6/21/88)

They buried him today
On the hill
Just above Prestonsburg

I remember going there
Twice before
To bury grandpaw and Jean

That was 19 years ago
People I love
Have been dying and going for a long time

I watched the others
And I tried to find him
In their eyes

I loved them
For loving him

I wanted to scream
 "Daddy"
  "Daddy"
   "I'm sorry, Daddy"

I wanted to reach him.
But there was no way to him anymore
Home was just a white house on the farm
No one goes there anymore

Now it is 13 years later
I buried him today.
If I were to write a thousand books
In his name, would it matter now?
I can't give him anything anymore.

But I can give me everything————
             (Rose Hall Warnke)

They Did the Best They Knew How

If he were alive today, it would make my father so very sad to read just the few, terrible pains I have written about — the pains I felt as I was growing up with my family and other outside primary caretakers.

How sad it is to remind my mother of what she already knows. Yet, it is impossible to understand the present and to go into the future in a healthy, positive way without dealing with the past. I must feel and deal with those awful past pains. I have lived in pain and denial far too long. My life has been full of pain and depression, leaving me feeling unfulfilled. I have ignored and tolerated my pains for too long a time.

Therefore, I choose to reveal just some of those hurts to you. I hope this will enable you to see me better. I have chosen to reveal them to myself so that I can recover and see myself better. In so doing, just maybe, you will begin to see yourself better, and to know the hope that awaits all of us.

I am a grown adult woman now. I am learning that I am capable of so much more than I was ever aware of before.

I am also a grown adult woman in recovery. And it is essential to my recovery to learn unconditional acceptance of others and to learn unconditional accept-ance of myself. This is the key to your recovery as well.

All of the degradations, humiliations, criticisms, verbal abuses, emotional annihilations — they were real. They were destructive, they were painful — but they are also over! They were yesterday.

And today is not yesterday — today is not tomorrow.

Today is today:

Therefore do not be anxious for tomorrow; for tomorrow will care for itself. Each day has enough trouble of its own. (Matt. 6:34)

My pain — remembered today — can become almost debilitating if I don't put it into its proper perspective. It has been a factor — one factor — in ending my marriage. In fact, it has been a factor in ending most of my ill-attempted intimate relationships.

If my father were alive and here today what would I say to him? I would thank him. I would tell him how very much I love him. I would tell him how much I wish he and I could have known each other better while I was growing up, and especially now.

I would talk with him about all the lonely, abandoned times I felt when he was gone. I would speak with him about how scared I was, and tell him how much I wanted him to hold me in his lap and make me feel safe.

And I would tell him how much I needed and wanted to know that he would always be there, and never leave me. I would let him know how awful it was to feel so angry and alone, and not to understand why. I would ask him if he had any idea that I needed him so much. I needed his approval, his kind touch, his laughter, his smile, his comfort, his strength, his way of always saying such funny things at the most inappropriate times. I needed his love as a father. I needed his time.

I would let him know that now I understand why he was driven to work so hard and to be gone all the time — and how he could only be who he was even though it was so painful to me — to all of us. I would let him know. . . .

Because, you see, I do understand. I realize and know that the way he behaved and taught me was how he had been treated and taught as a child. This did not make him less responsible for me — it's just that now

I am able to see how we carry, without even realizing it, the terrible wrong ways of hearing and acting from our childhoods into our adulthoods and then on further to our children.

And, if we do not pass on our dysfunctional ways to our children, we express them in society — in our schoolrooms, our courts, our entire lives and relationships.

And still, all the parenting failures of my father did not negate his success. It did not leave him naked, with nothing good in my eyes.

I am able to see. . . for the first time.

I am able to remember correctly the good things. . . .

I am able to forgive. . . and. . . I do not want to forget.

Forgetting would rob me of very crucial parts of myself and my past. I must not forget anything. For it is all my past that has brought me to this place within myself. ALL of my past — into this place called today.

As for my mother, thankfully, she is still living. She is touchable. She is not far from me in my heart. She is not far from me in distance. I have the opportunity to express and communicate my love to her.

Beginning to grow up these past few years — and continuing to grow up — have allowed me an insight and wisdom about life that I could never have had without this "ALL PAST" I speak about.

Now it is also easier to see and know my mother...by looking back into her time of growing up in eastern Kentucky, as a little girl in the early 1900's.

How she managed to endure her many losses...the abandonments...the tragic blows of life that began for her at age twelve...the loneliness...the very idea of just having children of her own.

At age twelve mother lost her younger sister who was only six years old...soon after that her mother died in childbirth and so did the baby. The family was left with my mother, her father, her younger sister and brother. Being the oldest of the children, my mother felt she had to assume the role of surrogate mother.

Eventually she was placed with a relative until she was older. Her father moved away. It is unclear to me what happened to her brother and sister during this period. In fact, all of these circumstances are unclear to me. Mother, understandably, does not like to talk about those painful times very much.

Within a few years, her father remarried. Her sister also married and soon thereafter her sister died at age twenty in childbirth and the baby died also. Within a period of ten to twelve years, she experienced five close family deaths and the remarriage of her father who also fathered another son. All of this happened after she was moved from her familiar home and before she had time to recover from the loss of her mother.

There is so much more I could go into but this book is not about my mother's tragic past. It is about understanding and forgiveness. It is also about how our negative, abusive past experiences are carried into our lives, contaminating our behavior and possibly destroying us and our relationships.

This same cycle exists in many families. Abusive patterns are often perpetuated from one generation to the next. Through prayer you will be able to understand how these patterns may be influencing your behavior, and through prayer you will be able to accept and to forgive. This is how freedom comes to the human soul.

I can now recognize how both of my parents, and many other family members, have suffered deeply. And I am certain the same must be true of their families before them, and before them, and before them, as each inherited the pains that were passed down from preceding generations.

Please understand that the point in all of this is not to suggest that we should dig around in the past just to dredge up old pains and abuses and to carry them around like excess baggage. The goal is to become whole, healthy individuals. And this is not possible without forgiveness and Jesus.

The road to recovery can be long, hard and it may continue throughout our lives. It can also be an adventure of sorts. Life can be celebrated each time a new door of understanding is opened and then gently closed correctly. It is a matter of how we choose to go about achieving a better way.

I am choosing to celebrate my life, to praise God for what He has and is doing. I choose not to question Him or others for what they did or did not do.

Above all, I choose to break the cycle of pain!

My mother is a remarkable woman in her late seventies. She is vibrant. She is very active even though she has many major health problems that have existed for many years. She is thoughtful, and sometimes she is thoughtless. She has chosen to live alone since the death of my father. All of her family members passed away early except for her half-brother and a nephew. She has become a wonderful, caring person even though she is sometimes still difficult to please.

It is no longer necessary for me just to tolerate her; now I enjoy her.

More importantly, I love her deeply. I grieve dearly for her past, perhaps sometimes more than my own, and I am still trying to learn how to let her know. We are able to communicate now — even when we disagree.

Mother has learned a valuable secret to my inner being, and possibly to the inner beings of all mankind. She expressed this understanding to me recently: "Honey, I have just realized something."

"Yes," I responded, "and what is it?"

"Well," she said, "I have just realized that when you are not doing very well, you stay to yourself and I don't get to see you. So, why don't you just come over and sit with me awhile. We don't have to talk or do anything, we'll just sit together."

In other words, we will just be!

How many years have I been seeking answers to myself, running from that something, hiding from that something, confused about who I am...and now we both understand.

IT IS ENOUGH TO JUST BE!

No, I do not regret not having learned that before now...nor do I regret her not being able to teach me...it is enough that we both know it now!

And I refuse to allow those abusive contaminations from my past to continue to contaminate my present and ultimately my future and the futures of my children and their children, my grandchildren.

Yes, I must say thank you to my mother and father and to all my former caretakers. Thank you for then and thank you for now!

I have a wonderful life ahead. I can now be my own safe, loving, healthy caregiver! And you can choose to take better care of YOU!

I Sang Songs

Not that it matters now
But I was 36 then.
He was 33.
I was from private schools
*   and canopy beds*

He fell in love with me,
Not in the way men fall in love with women,
But in the way
Little boys fall in love with their mothers.

I brought him homemade chicken noodle soup
And gave him vitamins

He gave me beautiful things
He gave me time.

He could not give me himself!
Everything was for the first time,
Again
And again
I composed and played and sang songs
Into microphones to him
He told funny stories
To a lady
Somewhere
Who never sang to him.

All through the first years
We celebrated ourselves,
Spread our feelings as we knew then
Across the United States, New Zealand, and
Canada
And then, in November, he received a letter
And left me there,
Like a rainy concert.

Even after, I had been noticed
By others,
I could still hear the sound of him
Not being there.

It's 12 years later
And now
I sing and play songs into microphones
Not to you — or to me-----

I sing my songs for
   Myself-----my lost self.

I sing my songs for
    Myself————my found self.

(Rose Hall Warnke)

Mike:

I only exist in a round ball of yellow light. I'm a face on a poster, or an image on video tape. No one really knows me, and no one really wants to. Even some of the people closest to me stay away from any sort of inner knowledge, because I think they are afraid of what lies down there — real deep.

How could I have done all those things I did in the past before I met Jesus? Somewhere down deep inside of me there is a "not-too-pleasing" being. I think — even if subconsciously — my past leaves tracks on the minds of my friends. I know it has left tracks on me.

Dysfunctional — that's a term I've learned lately in counseling. I've even learned what it means. It means you are broken. Something about you doesn't work. A lot of the time, whatever was broken was wrecked a long time ago — in your childhood, in all probability. And the breaking may have been so traumatic that the only way to live with it was to hide. Like when you broke your mom's best vase and hid the shards in the coal bin in the hopes that no one would even notice it was missing.

You can hide things for a while, maybe even a great while, but sooner or later, whatever it is will work its way to the surface like a splinter in your thumb that's left unattended. But by the time it does, you have to deal with the festering too. Not too many people are willing to chance an infection of their own, just for a close look at yours.

After a time of trying to cross over the line of trying to show your real self to people who say they are there for you, and having those people turn away in disgust, you learn to just keep it to yourself. Every once in a while, you get fooled. You want to believe so badly! And always you wind up at the same place. Because part of the dysfunction is to always choose to reach out to those who will do to you what you fear most! Does this sound insane? It can be!

Isn't it odd for a person with my sort of public recognition to feel worthless? Isn't it funny that someone who stands in front of thousands of people, who are screaming his name every night, should feel so alone? That I have, more than once, thought the only way out is to die? The pain can be so great when you're trapped that you'd be willing to chew your leg off just to get away!

People will say, "But none of it is real. Just turn it over to Jesus. Stop being such a wimp and get yourself together!" It's easy to explain fire when your clothes aren't in flames!

Another popular line I've often heard is, "You shouldn't feel like that." I always want to respond to that one with, "Well, then, how should I feel? And if this isn't the way, then what is? If I've chosen the wrong direction and made the wrong choices because that was all I knew to do, then would somebody please tell me what is right and do for me what is necessary to ease my pain?"

The answer is No! Even if willing, no one can. It's not up to others; it's up to you! They can't, you must. And looking to them instead of to yourself sets everyone up for a failed relationship. Friends, spouse, children — everybody! And many, many times, the breaking is permanent. Especially when the other is as broken and hidden as you.

I've tried to find people who could make me happy. Not just I-can-deal-with-the-pain happy, I'll-get-by happy, but "Ozzie and Harriet" happy. Ward-and-June-Cleaver happy. "Life With Riley" happy. "Father Knows Best" happy. Happy — perfectly happy. To put those kinds of expectations on others is not only unfair, it's downright cruel! And the worst kind of cruelty is the kind you don't mean.

I was cruel to Rose. I didn't mean to be, but I was. I did and said things to manipulate our relationship, so that I could receive what I was looking for without realizing that I was drawing a line through much of what was scarred and painful in her. My very nature dredged up all sorts of monsters for her, and it wasn't long before I'd earned her mistrust and suspicion. Until, as she often said, "The only way I can deal with my pain is to get away from the cause of it!" And the object of her disaffection was *me*. She just didn't believe me anymore. I had said, "I'll change" so many times. Change into what I thought she wanted, so that she would repay me by being what I needed.

I couldn't change. I didn't know how. I may not have even wanted to. Being so used to the way I was, maybe being new scared me more than living with the pain I was accustomed to and had learned to expect.

All I know for sure is that Rose took none of this lying down. She fought, she cried, she did everything she could think of to save herself, and I matched her stride for stride.

Don't Do This
Do This
Watch What You Say
Say What You Think
Be Close
Stay Away
Fight
Make Peace
Cry
Scream
Rage
Roll Over
Sit Up
Play Dead
Join the Circus and See the Clowns!

"Well, if you know all this stuff, what's the problem?" I know it *now!* After eleven years of massive pain and disappointment. After countless lines crossed and corners turned. After many, many points of no return.

For the last few years we have lived virtually separated, and for the last two years, literally separated. Bound by responsibility and not much else. Mutual regard remains — and at least we stopped the anger before it turned to hate. We don't want bad for one another, only good. We have a strange sort of friendship, one I know I rely on in many ways.

It is this friendship and regard that has helped us not only to build a ministry, but to determine that no matter what happens in our personal lives, to keep that ministry together!

There is a prevalent idea in the body of Christ that once the "unpardonable sin" (divorce) has been committed then everything else just automatically gets trashed. Well, I don't buy that! "The gifts and callings of God are without repentance," and God is not sorry He called me and I'm not sorry He did either. And because I'm not perfect, I love Him and want to serve Him all the more.

I can't be the only imperfect person in the world. And if that's true, the others probably need ministry as much as perfect people do. Who would be better at providing that ministry than a broken soldier? At least, it helps me to understand where others are coming from. A lot of people don't want the flawed ones, but they don't bother me. I know them. And what I learn as I go along, maybe I can give to them — to you.

Love and tears and a big heart are things God has given me in abundance. And from them He has shown a way to make people happy, at least for a while. It may not be much of a calling, but it's mine.

The music that Rose makes is the most uplifting, thought-provoking I have ever heard. There is no reason that her music should stop just because unlooked-for problems have occurred in her life. Rose ministers to the battered and the bruised. Prison is one of the places where God has led her to find them. And a heart like that can't just stop because things aren't perfect. She won't quit just because people think she should. I know her. She has a calling from God and it doesn't depend on anyone but her and the Lord. Her writing, her music, her life — all of these reflect this. She's had a lot of road blocks thrown in her path over the years, and never once has she pulled to the side of the road and given up. Maybe some of the side trips have been a little weird, but she never gave up.

So here we go. We're not hiding. We are looking ahead and trusting God and our friends to make it all work. Thank you — in advance.

Editor:

Woven throughout this chapter is one important theme: personal responsibility. I appreciate the mature manner with which Mike and Rose face their problems.

Yes, they were both abused. As Mike points out, they were even dysfunctional. But neither one of them seeks to remain in the role of victim.

They are assuming individual, personal responsibility for their lives. They are not engaging in blame-shifting, as if to say that their parents or others have caused their problems.

Loneliness? Yes, they both know how that feels. But instead of feeling stuck in a swamp of self-pity, all alone, they are reaching out to others through this book, concerts, personal ministry, music, etc. This is a healthy way to deal with one's problems.

As Mike suggests, the pain and brokenness of their lives enables them to reach out to others with greater compassion and comfort. This is a biblical approach, as the following passage from Second Corinthians 1:3,4 reveals:

> Praise be to the God and Father of our Lord Jesus Christ, the Father of compassion and the God of all comfort, who comforts us in all our troubles, so that we can comfort those in any trouble with the comfort we ourselves have received from God.

You may not be ready to take this step in your life at this point. That's okay. There is hope in simply realizing that there is a purpose in all that you are going through. It will make you stronger. You will be better prepared to help others as a result of all you are going through.

One of the areas of personal responsibility that is of obvious importance to Mike and Rose at the present time involves being true to themselves. This is such a vital part of the recovery process. Each of us needs to learn who we are, what we believe in and what our values are.

This cannot be second-hand knowledge, for each of us is responsible for sorting these things our by ourselves, for ourselves. Many of our problems stem from the fact that we may not be true to ourselves. We need to ask ourselves the following questions:

Am I living in accord with my values?
Do I practice my beliefs?
Do I know what my personal beliefs and values
    are?
Are the convictions I express so strongly really
    my own or did they come from someone else?

Many times, some of the most severe personal problems we experience are the result of us not knowing either what our beliefs and values are or not living in accord with them.

We are responsible for practicing what we believe and living according to our values. To do so is to be congruent on the outside with what we are on the inside. Not to do so is injurious to ourselves and others.

As Rose points out, life is a series of choices. We can choose to forgive others and ourselves. We can choose to take care of ourselves. We can choose to be real. We can choose to accept the unchangeable past. We can choose to celebrate our lives. For healing and recovery to come to us, we must indeed make these choices.

7
What Do I Do With the Anger?

The true way is to tell God exactly what I feel. He knows anyway! If I feel that God shouldn't have allowed me to be so treated I might as well say it and have the relief from getting it out of my system. He is already aware that I feel that way so I might as well be honest. . . . Things like a hard dig in the garden. . . or a vigorous walk all help — but to let it all come out before our understanding and unshockable heavenly Father is still the best way.

(Gaven Reid — *A New Happiness*)

Mike:

Some days it is much easier to do this writing than it is on other days. There are times when I am so angry that it is hard to be fair about what I have to say. At other times, I'm so sorry for the things that I've done wrong, that I want to blame myself for the whole thing. It can be very hard to keep a balance.

The tendency is for the couple involved in divorce to engage in an orgy of pointing the blame at the other person so that they can feel better about themselves. At such a time, it's also important to look good in the eyes of other people. As a matter of fact, looking good to the friends and family can get to be the most important factor of all. That's when the children often become weapons instead of just the kids.

In a divorce, children go through a huge amount of emotional turmoil. Putting them in the middle is absolutely unfair. Trying to make them choose which parent to love and which to hate, which to keep and which to throw away, can cause scars that will never go away. They will go through enough of this sort of thing on their own, without being asked to by their folks. Rose and I have decided to do our best not to let this happen. It's not always easy, but we try.

On the days when anger is all I can feel, I try to keep it to myself, or talk it over with Dr. John, my counselor. When it does slop over, it usually slops over on Rose. I don't like to fight with her. Fighting has been too much of our relationship. I didn't like it then, and I don't like it any better now. Dr. John says that it's to be expected, but that doesn't make it any easier to take. I have a temper. It's been one of the things I did most wrong. It makes me stubborn. I don't listen; I just want to be heard. That's one of the things I did most wrong too.

Rose fights back! She is not what you would call a passive person! She would fight a grizzly bear with a fly swatter if she needed to — and she would win! She never took any of my guff lying down. We had frequent, loud, prolonged arguments. Sometimes Rose tried to walk away, but I would never let her. I would often follow her around the house, insisting that we fight it out. I wanted to get it over with, but to her I was just being insensitive. She would finally get to the place where she was ready to pull her hair out —

or mine — depending on which was the handiest. Her life had been full of this kind of abuse since the beginning of her childhood. I didn't know about "triggers" then. (A trigger is a button one pushes that causes a reaction in the other person — like sticking your hand in another person's wound, causing pain.) If I had known about "triggers," maybe it would have meant something to me. I'm not sure. I have plenty of triggers of my own.

Rose, for her part, was somewhat of an unknown to me. In lots of ways, she frightened me. Her background, her family — all of this was alien to me. She was raised with a sense of social position. She spent her Saturdays learning to serve tea; I spent mine playing in a wrecked car behind my father's truck stop.

Don't get me wrong. Rose is not a social snob. She rebelled against all of this stuff at a very early stage in her life. The result was alienation from her family and the need to try to raise two small babies on her own. And that's just what she did. She made a load of mistakes, but she did it nonetheless. It made her tough — not hard — but self-reliant. A strong woman. Still vulnerable underneath, still able to be hurt, but on the surface, very able to cope with whatever life was willing to dish out. This can be very intimidating to someone who is as insecure as I can be.

Because of her scars and other aspects of her personality, I never knew just what was going to start an argument. I found myself in the middle of an ongoing confrontation that I had absolutely no idea how to deal with. When I did discover that this or that thing was a problem, I tried to change myself to accommodate the situation. It never worked, I believe, for two reasons:

1. Accommodation is not real change. What has to happen is to try to understand the underlying problems, rather than just making cosmetic changes. (That's like trying to treat cancer with a wash rag.)

2. Some of the changes that were really needed involved basic character traits that I didn't even know I had, much less know how to deal with. I tried and failed. I tried and failed, and finally I just quit trying. The gap between us became complete.

In order to avoid the pain, Rose went her way and I went mine. There were brief flashes of hope, but for the most part, we just stayed away from one another. We occupied the same space, but we didn't have much in common except the ministry. That we did well. I had respect for her professional sense, and she had the same kind of respect for me. We worked, but we didn't play. I felt rejected and unwanted in a personal way. I was deadly hurt. Not only did this hurt live in the now of my life, but it also brought back to me all the times when I had been rejected and hurt in the past. Not only was I living Rose's and my situation, but every situation in my life that had caused me pain.

"Why didn't you talk about it?"

I didn't know how. And by the time I had learned, there was nothing left to talk about, because it had gone on too long. It had caused too much pain. Other factors had taken us past the point of repairing what had been

been destroyed between us. The best we had left was to learn to be friends — for us, for our kids, and for *you.*

The ministry that God has given us has meant a lot to a great many people. And through all this we have tried to keep all of you in mind. We don't want what we're going through to take away from our ability to minister to the people who need us.

I'm sure that there will be those who think I am just interested in "saving my butt." Twenty years in ministry is a long time, and it is true that starting over now (in something else) would be a real problem. But I have never been in the ministry because it's all I had to do. I have been in the ministry because it's all I could do.

I have my education, and there are many things that I could do with my life if God would let me. But up to this point, that hasn't been the case.

I tried to quit once, but the Lord got my attention in no uncertain terms. He spoke to me. Maybe twice in my life I have heard what I believe was the audible voice of God, and this was one of those occasions. Foolishly, I had given the Lord an ultimatum: "Either you show me a sign or I'm through!" He answered me with a similar challenge: *"Either you minister, or you die!"* He told me that He had not brought me through all that He had just so I could give up when the going got rough. He told me that I could either follow in the calling He's put on my life, or He would take me home. Now, going home doesn't sound so bad some times, but how could I face Him and eternity, knowing that I had been too much of a coward to fulfill my commission? And just so no one things that I'm coming up with this now just to make everyone feel sorry for me, this took place over fifteen years ago. This was at the top of my "Reasons to Live List" that I referred to earlier.

Rose has the same conviction not to quit. She and I both feel that our personal situation does not alter the fact that we have a ministry that God intends for us to carry on. It may even be that we have more to share now than we did before. More compassion, more understanding, more sympathy for the failures of others. There are a lot of people whose lives have been trashed by situations similar to ours. If what we have learned from all this helps others, then the Scriptures have been proven right again. "And we know that in all things God works for the good of those who love him, who have been called according to his purpose" (Rom. 8:28).

Rose:

Lord, grant that I may avoid useless quarrels that tire and wound without achieving results. Keep me from those angry outbursts that draw attention but leave one uselessly weakened. Keep me from wanting always to outstrip others in my conceit, crushing those in my way. Wipe from my face the look of dark, dominating anger. Rather, Lord, grant that I may live my days calmly and fully, as the sea slowly covers the whole shore. Make me humble like the sea, as, silently and gently, it spreads out, unnoticed. May I wait for my

brothers and match my pace to theirs, that I
may move upward with them.
(Michael Quoist — *Prayers of Life*)

You name the emotion. I've been through it.
Anger. Rage. Terror. Panic. Anxiety. Fear. Depression.
I've felt them all. Sometimes, even, all at once. The
trouble with all of them, of course, is that they are self-
defeating and self-destructive. When we turn these
kinds of feelings inward, they always lead to gloom,
despair and depression. Always.

While I want to acknowledge the dark side of
divorce as the painful reality it is, I also want to
emphasize hope in this book. I want you to be
challenged as I was to find hope in the midst of your
depression and despair. This will make you feel
confused — and angry. It will open your heart to
question and to feel pain. It is a painful work indeed,
but it is your work; it is your much-needed work.

I am praying for you. As you read and feel, you
may not always understand Michael and me. I hope
you will be able, at least, to accept us, and through this
acceptance, to know our love for you.

I never dreamed that I would one day write a book
about divorce — certainly not my own divorce! As a
matter of fact, I had written about divorce in my
previous book:

> Divorce can happen to anyone. But, there is
> no way that anyone could convince me that
> two people, who have made Christ the Lord

of their life, and are fully committed to each other, could give up a marriage and go through a divorce. I urge you to make that commitment to your husband or wife and to your Christ. Make Christ the Lord of your life — not just Saviour.

Now I am writing to say I understand. It's so easy to make pronouncements for the lives of others. To set rules for others to follow. To judge those who don't, won't or can't comply. Jesus, who is my Savior and Lord, is showing me how to avoid those pitfalls.

Yes, Michael and I are Christians, and we are writing a book about our own painful divorce. It is also a book about two mangled childhoods from two completely opposite walks of life. The pain — the suffering — the results — are the same.

I hope you can be compassionate. I hope you will not judge us. And, as you wonder why I would even attempt to write such a book as this, know that it is for you as well as it is for me and for us.

It is often said that most (if not all) families are dysfunctional in some sense or another. John Bradshaw, best-selling author of *Homecoming* and *The Family,* has stated that 100% of families are dysfunctional at some level. About half of all marriages end in divorce (including Christian marriages!). One of every four girls and one of every ten boys are sexually molested before the age of eighteen. (Thousands more are abused in other ways.)

Our awareness of child abuse — people abuse — is reaching mind-boggling proportions. With the greater knowledge of these horrifying human failures, is it not possible to be better able to stop them?

Remains

The way he moves
The way he gives me words
  To go through the day with

Do we inherit thoughts
From other times?
  Other faces————other minds?

Surely he learned how to
  Love me
By being loved
  By someone else————

Surely he learned how to
  Hurt me
By being hurt
  By someone else————

Surely when we realize why
  We do as we do
We can make it better
  For each other————
                    (Rose Hall Warnke)

Poetry For My Memory

My memory is gentle
  about you,
Mixed with anger and hurt.

It wasn't always
    that way.
There was a time I couldn't feel.

There will come a new way
    of feeling.
By taking care of me, as well as you.

Then my gifts to you
    will be many
        Like honesty
        And understanding
            And the truer parts of me.

We're a special person
    You and me
    The kind that never happens
        And has.

(Rose Hall Warnke)

It is not, and was not, our Lord's intention for us to use His creation to make human rubble. And yet, as we fail and we make that human rubble, it is from the ruins that He can rebuild magnificent human beings. In fact, it is from those depths of misery that we can learn to become compassionate, gracious, victorious creatures in His name.

As you learn about Michael and me — our successes and our failures — I want you to grow. I want you to see us as we really are — to truly know us. Perhaps that will help you to know yourself, to understand yourself better.

Wad some power the Giftie gie us,
To see oursel's as others see us.
(Robert Burns)

Being a Christian has not made me immune from sin (as I had erroneously expected). Getting married to Michael did not make me invulnerable to the stresses and strains of a modern marriage.

Being a human Christian, on the other hand, has made me know who I am! My Christian journey has taught me how to love and that I must not judge! And although I know these things, His forgiving love continues to teach me that I am a human being. Even though I might like to be God, and others would like to be God — I am not God; we are not God!

The most important lesson of all that I've learned is: when I fail, Jesus will be victorious!

Must we, when we fall, continue to lie down? No. Never. Absolutely not.

Though I was never taught how to communicate my thoughts and feelings, I am determined to make up for lost time! At one time I was denied the privilege of feeling my feelings; now I can feel them, know them and share them! Once, I was able only to expel information (on a cognitive level); now I can share my experiences openly and honestly. Writing this book is one of the greatest challenges I've faced in forty-seven years. I welcome this opportunity and I embrace it, realizing that Jesus Christ does give victory over all our problems.

This is meant to be a book of hope. A statement of victory. An honest portrayal of our human struggle.

What do we do with our anger, our guilt, our fear? We turn it over to the One who inspired these words:

> I remember my affliction and my wandering, the bitterness and the gall. I well remember them, and my soul is downcast within me. Yet this I call to mind and therefore I have hope: Because of the Lord's great love we are not consumed, for his compassions never fail. They are new every morning; great is your faithfulness.... The Lord is good to those whose hope is in him, to the one who seeks him.
>
> (Lam. 3:19-25)

Where Is Love?

Love does not live
In the mind
Unless
The mind is your home

Breath does not mean you're alive
Unless
You have so little life
Breath is all
You have

Life isn't always a game
Unless
Games are your life.

Love does not live
In the mind
Unless
The mind is your home.
(Rose Hall Warnke)

Editor:

Most often we give vent to our anger by engaging in arguments and quarrels. When true communication has broken down, such verbal "fights" usually result.

As everyone knows, quarrels do not accomplish anything other than the venting of our anger and resentment. Most argumentative statements are judgmental in tone and they usually begin with "you messages." "*You* are no good." "*You* are the cause of all this." "*You* will never change," "Why do *you* always...?" etc.

More effective communication involves "I messages." "*I* feel hurt when you don't remember our anniversary." "*I* have the right to make my own decisions." "*I* will not accept your judgment," etc.

When another person attempts to pull a trigger of guilt or fear in your life, he or she is trying to manipulate you. Quite often, the goal is to make you feel so badly about something that you will do what your accuser says. This is manipulation, and it is abuse.

As Eleanor Roosevelt once observed, "No one can make you feel inferior without your permission." Put-downs and critical judgments serve no useful purpose. They come from an individual's need to have power over another person, total control of another's thoughts, feelings and life. It is counter-productive to engage in such behavior and it is self-defeating to let another do this to you.

The core dimensions of an effective interpersonal relationship, as outlined by Dr. Carl Rogers, are: empathy (the ability to feel what the other person is feeling), unconditional positive regard (love without judgment and with no strings attached), genuineness and warmth. In an atmosphere of such love and acceptance, an individual or two people living together, can grow and mature in vitally positive ways. This is possible only when both partners in a relationship are committed to that goal.

When you find yourself in a relationship in which you would like to maintain that commitment but your partner is unwilling to do so, do not revert back to ineffective patterns of manipulation. Identify the behaviors that each of you engage in that weaken your relationship, then look for ways to avoid those behaviors. Some emotional detachment is called for, not letting the other's words and actions pull triggers of emotional responses in your life.

Even if only one person begins to deal with the relationship on an adult level, positive change is likely to result in the relationship because the other will be likely to adjust his or her behavior accordingly.

You can change your responses, and in so doing, your spouse may see the need to change his or hers.

8

The Fallen Have a Future

For we do not have a high priest who cannot sympathize with our weaknesses, but one who has been tempted in all things as we are, yet without sin. Let us therefore draw near with confidence to the throne of grace, that we may receive mercy and may find grace to help in time of need (Heb. 4:15-16).

Rose:

It is June now. Three months of writing and growing and healing and worrying and crying have passed since I last took pen in hand to attempt this most-difficult project. Those months passed ever so slowly, and yet, also very quickly.

Three months of growth have gone by. Three months of more grief and pain have also passed. And so, I continue this silent journey — day by day, hour by hour.

The agony of our divorce does not go away. It does not become more bearable. It does not change. Does time heal all wounds?

I feel a need to ignore that agony, but I can't. I have a desperate wish, a deep desire to ignore it, to avoid it, to deny it. Along with all of those turbulent emotions, I want to be able to explain it. Will anyone understand? Do even I understand it? The ongoing, aching search to understand it is part of what keeps me going.

But none of the pain goes away.

Today, I am seeking to understand forgiveness. I seek forgiveness itself! I'm sure you understand that no further explanation is necessary.

Today, I travel toward the future. I am trying to exercise my faith more. Today, I am able to travel forward with more trust, more determination, more desire to deepen my relationship with Jesus, my Savior. Today, I am reaching for tomorrow!

Today, my faith does not fail me — even though I fail me. And others fail me. Somehow, there is a comfort in knowing all of us do fail — and I still wish it wasn't so.

Now is the time for me to present my failure to Jesus. I turn to Him again, and I am reminded that His love for me is from everlasting to everlasting. His love — so extraordinary, yet so simple. A perfect love without any conditions! Now is the time — an amazing opportunity — to feel, to know, to remember who is the Greatest.

One of my problems is that I have always been a driven and controlled woman. Driven by my circumstances, my family, my friends, my co-workers. Driven by my needs, my desires, and mostly — driven by myself!

To take it one step further, I have oftentimes been controlled by my needs, my past and my falsely learned beliefs that if I work hard enough, work long enough, go to enough places, gain enough knowledge, read enough books, surely I will not fail. Surely I will not disappoint anyone!

Yes, driven, controlled, and manipulated by false beliefs that I am in control — that we humans have the last say! We are prone to believe that we can have the last say, and we can, if that is the way we choose to run our lives. Through all that I've gone through, I've discovered that such an approach to life simply does not work.

Once, during a counseling session, I listened to a young woman as she spoke about her fears and doubts. It frightened me to hear of her unhappiness and despair because my own life and pain so closely paralleled hers.

Is divorce a sin? Yes.

Is Jesus my Savior? Yes. He is so much bigger than our finite minds believe Him to be. Oh yes, I do know Jesus! I know Him well. At the same time, however, I realize I do not know Jesus.

It is a strange dichotomy, isn't it? I have faith and I don't have faith. I trust and yet I don't know how to trust. I hope and I despair. Through it all, though, one thing remains certain — and crystal-clear — I have never fully realized that Jesus has known and does know me.

He knows my pain. He knows my despair. He knows my fears. He knows of my torment, my disconnected, semi-conscious, murdered soul!

I have traveled this earth for years living in a glass bubble — gazing in amazement eagerly at the confusion of those around me — and in me!

While I have desperately sought to fill up the spiritual emptiness within me, I have also sought to deny that emptiness. It is a hole, if you will, that only He can fill. Nothing but Him and the healing of my soul can fill the hole, that was caused by my murdered inner child and my wounded spirit.

I have hated the pains and sins of this world with a passion. That passion has been so great that I have often found myself setting out to help resolve the hurts and pains of humanity! This passion has been both a bane and a blessing for me. On the one hand, it has given me something to live for; on the other, it has led me down some dark paths of frustration. Ultimately, however, I believe my passion to see healing effected in the lives of others will lead to my own healing.

When one learns to hate the sins of mankind, it is easy to cross over the thin line between what one is and what one does, resulting in hatred for the sinner as well as the sin. That certainly happened to me when I faced my own sin; I began to hate myself!

That self-hatred grew and it seeped deeply into my heart. It begins in the mind — in the form of guilty thoughts — then the seepage contaminates the heart. From mind to heart, from heart to mind — a vicious cycle of a silent disease known as hatred — hatred of self, of sin, of weakness, of failure, of everything and everyone.

Let me say simply: Life becomes unbearable with hate.

Anger, bitterness, resentment, fear, condemnation, selfish ambitions, arrogance — the all-powerful ego — they all became my failures. They were MY SINS. They led me to divorce. They became *me*! They created in me a false self.

How very easy it is to fall into the treacherous hands of the "False Self" when you do not know who you are. The "False Self" is readily awaiting to guide us — even teach us. Then, it speeds us to our ready fall.

In one way or another, each of us has fallen or is headed for a fall. We must all fail and we must all fall. Sooner or later, it happens to each of us. Some of us will fall more than once — more than twice — even constantly! Many times seems to be the average for most of us.

Jesus spoke to Peter (calling him "Simon") in Luke 22:31-34: "Simon, Simon, behold, Satan has demanded permission to sift you like wheat; but I have prayed for you, that your faith may not fail; and you, when once you have turned again, strengthen your brothers."

Jesus knew Peter would deny Him three times, and told him so. Still, Jesus said, "When once you have turned again, strengthen your brothers...."

James Robinson said, "Most of us will fail, and all of us fail in some way. Yet we can turn once again back to Jesus and know who is the greatest. And still, by the sufficient grace of God, the fallen have a future."

Will my faith sustain me while I fall? I pray it will.

Can I look to the future while I stand in the mire of today?

Is my God so loving that He will look with me into the future while standing in my failures with me today?

I believe He is!

Divorce is a sin! And we have failed!

JESUS NEVER FAILS!

Mike:

Fully recognizing the sinfulness of divorce, I find myself wondering at the same time if living a lie is not a greater sin. For several years, I was living a lie in my marriage.

I do know that honesty is not a sin. Jesus said, "Then you will know the truth, and the truth will set you free" (John 8:32).

The truth was that our marriage wasn't working. Nothing we did could fix it. Our dysfunctional personalities militated against our marriage ever working out.

Even as I write these words, there is a measure of freedom coming to my spirit. Someone once wrote, "We're only as sick as our secrets." And the secret about my dysfunctional marriage was eating me alive! It was consuming all my thoughts and feelings. It was eroding my health and my ministry.

Confession is good for the soul. As I bare my soul to you, even now, I feel God's healing touch. James wrote, "Therefore confess your sins to each other and pray for each other so that you may be healed" (James 5:16).

As Rose and I confess our sins to you, we ask you to pray for us, that we may be healed. We know the truth of God's promise: "The prayer of a righteous man is powerful and effective" (James 5:16).

I want to guard against this chapter becoming a theological treatise. At the same time, however, I feel impelled to share certain insights God has given to me from His Word. One thing I've discovered is that sin is part and parcel of the human condition. "There is no difference, for all have sinned and fall short of the glory of God" (Rom. 3:23).

My divorce is just one of my many sins. The Apostle John wrote, "If we claim to be without sin, we deceive ourselves and the truth is not in us. If we confess our sins, he is faithful and just and will forgive us our sins and purify us from all unrighteousness. If we claim we have not sinned, we make him out to be a liar and his word has no place in our lives" (1 John 1:8-10).

This book is our confession. We are sinners. Our divorce is a sin. But thanks be to God, we are in recovery! God loves us. He is faithful and just to forgive us, and He is purifying us from all unrighteousness.

Sin, simply defined, is missing the mark. Our marriage has certainly missed the mark in more ways than one. But God has made provision for us — even in the sin of divorce: ". . . If anybody does sin, we have one who speaks to the Father in our defense — Jesus

Christ, the Righteous One. He is the atoning sacrifice for our sins, and not only for ours but also for the sins of the whole world" (1 John 2:1).

Yes, divorce is a sin. Our divorce is a sin. But it is not the unpardonable sin! God loves us. He forgives us. And I know He understands all that has happened in our lives.

When a person sins through anger or lust (or many other areas), he seldom purposely sets out to commit that sin. He does not say, for example, "Well, I think I will get angry at him or her. When I do, I know God will forgive me." There are premeditated sins, but, believe me, divorce is not one of them.

I don't know of any couple who got married with this thought in mind: "Well, I'll get married, but then I'll get divorced, and God will forgive me."

No. When most people get married, it is with the thought that the relationship will go on forever. When Rose and I got married, after an all-too-brief courtship, we had no thought of divorce, no plan that "if this doesn't work out, we'll get a divorce and God will forgive us." To have done that would have made our divorce (and our marriage) a premeditated sin, and it was not that at all.

To be perfectly truthful, I believed that my marriage to Rose would be a problem-solver. Perhaps that was my biggest mistake. I carried expectations into our relationship that it would have been impossible for any wife to fulfill.

I remember thinking in the early days of our marriage about how wonderful it would be to grow old with a beautiful, fun-loving, Christian woman like Rose.

Those were my thoughts; those were my plans. Neither of us set out to have a marriage that would end in divorce. Sin intervened, and as always, sin destroyed. It broke the marriage relationship irreparably. Although it is true that we let it happen, it is likewise true that it happened to us. From my point of view, we are victims of divorce rather than perpetrators of it.

When one goes through a tragedy, his eyes are opened to insights and understandings he never had before. In all likelihood, he might not have received these insights apart from the suffering. As one of my friends has pointed out, "Trouble always leads us to Jesus." In my own life, I can say that the troubled times I've faced in my marriage have helped me to understand the struggles others have so much more clearly. It has enhanced my ability to empathize with others. It has also drawn me ever closer to Jesus, ever closer to His mercy.

Some may think it's inappropriate, but I would like to close this chapter with a Bible verse I committed to memory many years ago:

> And we know that in all things
> God works for the good of those
> who love him, who have been called
> according to his purpose.
>
> (Rom. 8:28)

The Apostle Paul then goes on to say:

Who shall separate us from the love of Christ? Shall trouble or hardship or persecution or famine or nakedness or danger or sword? ...No, in all these things we are more than conquerors through him who loved us. For I am convinced that neither death nor live, neither angels nor demons, neither the present nor the future, nor any powers, neither height nor depth, nor anything else in all creation, will be able to separate us from the love of God that is in Christ Jesus our Lord.

(Rom. 8:35–39)

Not even divorce can separate Rose and me from that mighty love. God *is* working for our good.

And He is working His purposes out in your life as well. He loves you and He will help you.

Editor:

Mike touches on an important topic in this chapter when he mentions expectations and how they contribute to problems in a marriage. It is true that most of us carry expectations into a marriage with us. For the most part, these are expectations of what marriage should be like and expectations regarding how the husband and wife should act. A husband may expect his wife to behave in a certain way, and the wife may have expectations of her husband.

If these expectations are not clearly communicated at the outset, however, they become like land mines hidden in a field. The partners may not know where to step (how to behave) in a certain situation and the result is likely to be an unexpected explosion!

Again, the role of communication is of paramount importance. Many times we may not know we have these expectations ourselves. When this is the case, the help of a professional counselor should enable us to discover these hidden motivators more readily.

For example, Mike was expecting Rose to be his problem-solver. Since she didn't know that he had this expectation, she was unable to deal with it. In all likelihood, Mike didn't know that he had this expectation either until the counseling process revealed it to him.

The best way to communicate an expectation that we are aware of is with an I message: "I was hoping that you would have. . . ." Such a message is easy to respond to and it is facilitative (helpful) in nature.

The emphasis of this chapter is centered on the fact that the fallen do have a future. Both Mike and Rose acknowledge the failure of their marriage as being a sin. They do not attempt to justify it or to rationalize it away. At the same time, however, they are able to appropriate the forgiveness God promises to those who confess their sins.

"If we confess our sins, he is faithful and just and will forgive us our sins and purify us from all unrighteousness." (1 John 1:9).

9

Mike Warnke, the Preacher Vs. Mike Warnke, the Man

Rose:

Well, now, this should prove interesting — writing about the man who is going through a divorce with me!

A recent survey indicates that the most stressful "job" in the world is being a minister's wife! The third most stressful "job" is being a minister! After my experience, I find it easy to concur with both findings.

Actually, it has been quite hard for me to identify with Mike on the level of his being a preacher. I see him more as a man — the man who was my husband. When most people think of a preacher, they envision an individual who is above and beyond reproach. As regards the conduct and manners of a preacher, one expects him to be a model of decorum for the community to follow.

Well, that simply isn't Michael Alfred Warnke. His conduct and behavior are not always models of good manners and decorum. Please don't misunderstand me. Michael is a brilliant teacher. He has superior intelligence. His mind is of an academic turn. He holds

many degrees — too many, in fact, to even begin
discussing them.

His memory is staggering. For example, his ability
to recall details related to people he has met, books he
has read, events he has experienced is extraordinary.
He can tell you, in very confident words, the dates,
times, places, names, and all else of this nature, about
anyone he has studied in history. (And that is just about
everybody!) In fact, history is not the only area he can
expound on with great intelligence. (Just don't ever play
a game of trivia with him!)

As a theologian, he is outstanding. How do I
know? I have heard him debate, discuss and even argue
theology. We have yet to experience the full benefit
of Michael's biblical knowledge. (I'm sure we will one
day.) When a man is one of the greatest teachers, a
superior comedian, and an incredible overcomer, and
able to surmount all the obstacles he has faced as he
has gone forth to do God's will for more than twenty
years, I don't have any concern about him not fitting
the world's idea of a preacher.

You see, the labels we use are often insignificant.
It is the results that matter. God has used Michael, year
after year, concert after concert, to proclaim the Gospel.
As a result, thousands have left drugs, satanism, crime
and have come to Jesus. These wonderful people have
walked out of a dead past into a future that involves
the promise of heaven, the love of God, the salvation
of Jesus Christ, and an eternity with the Father.

Michael has been able to see these results because
he keeps on simply being himself. He doesn't put on

airs. He says what he thinks and feels. This is one of things I (and many others) respect about him. He's not some kind of special person; he's just a man who lives to tell you about Jesus — about hope — about love. he lives to tell you that God loves you — and very often he even tells you off!

This man, therefore, is not a preacher (at least not in the traditional sense). He is a human being who is not afraid — in fact, even desires — to let you see him as he is — flaws and all — as much as possible.

My father had many little sayings he liked to teach to his children. One of the sayings I remember most came from a popular song in the fifties. One of its lines went like this: "Before you criticize and abuse, walk a mile in my shoes, just walk a mile in my shoes. . . ."

I have never been able to walk anywhere in Michael's shoes, but I have been able to walk beside him — behind him — and even, sometimes, in front of him.

What I mean by all this is to say: When you have spent 300 or more days a year traveling around the world committed to just being able to say something to one person that would turn his heart from death to life, then you might be able to know a little about Michael. You might be able to understand him.

Michael, the preacher, versus Michael, the man? I still don't see him as a preacher. To me he is a man — a real-life human being. He is successful; he is a failure. He is strong; he is weak. He is young, yet he is old. He is good; he is bad. He is a clown; he is sad.

He is liberal; he is a conservative. He is brilliant; he is ignorant. He is real; he is false. He is honest; he lies.

He is a Peter — a David — a Thomas — a John. He is a father, a grandfather, and he has tried to be a husband. (That was, when he had the time — which wasn't very often.)

He is a best friend; he is a worst friend. He is giving and forgiving; he is selfish and unforgiving.

What is Michael Warnke really like? Are you getting the picture? He is human!!!

There are deep realms within Michael where no one will ever go — not even himself. Anyone who thinks they will be able to explore those areas with him — even if he tells them they can — are just kidding themselves.

I really know Michael. That knowledge is not based on having been allowed to know him, but it stems from the fact that I made him my life for twelve years. As I've tried to help Michael come to grips with some of his suppressed hurts and memories, I've discovered that it simply will not happen for me or for him or for anyone else on this earth.

When you come right down to it, is Michael really any different from me or you? Are there not those deep, dark places in all of us that we are unable and/or unwilling for anyone to visit for fear we might be destroyed?

Isn't it glorious of our Jesus that He not only knows those places, but He longs to make us understand how much he loves us, even with our dark, treacherous depths?

God is continually purifying and refining us so that we might become pure gold in His sight. Michael, like all the rest of us, is going through that process. God is not finished with us yet!

After living with Michael for more than a decade, I know that his heart is big enough to carry him through the worst of times. No matter what angers, frustrations, disappointments — no matter what horrible times we have put each other through and have gone through for each other — there is a place for us. It will be both a place alone and a place together.

All of the emotional crises and spiritual struggles of the past and present do not change the purpose of our lives. Both of us continue to go forward — to forge the raging waters of life, just to say again and again to anyone who wants to hear or needs to hear, "Jesus loves you just the way you are. Not the way you want to be, not the way others want you to be, not the way He knows you can be — but just the way you are."

How many times have we heard Michael say, "God didn't call you to be comfortable, He called you to be committed. He never said it would be easy; he said it would be worth it."

Michael, in some respects, is a mess! He eats the wrong foods, doesn't get proper rest, talks too much, doesn't talk about things he needs to enough, has no patience, has a frustrated temper, won't listen, is manipulating when he wants his way, suffers from deep childhood abuses, is offended easily, is overly emotional and sensitive — and these are just a few of his "messes."

Then, there's the other side of Michael. He is gentle, tender, and he is an incurable romantic. Forget it, if you ever think you going to get the best of him! (I mean, misuse him — it will never happen!) He has given away every watch I ever gave to him to a needy person, except for the one I finally had engraved with the date and a reference to a Father's Day gift!

So you can see, I could write an entire book about Michael. (And some day, maybe I will.)

I hope you understand Michael (and me) better after having read this chapter. I hope it leads you to love him.

May, 1991

If there is a time
When I'm alone again
Covered only with hands
That can never reach me.
If there is a time
Without him,
A time without hope of his ever coming back,

I could not cry
Because he's gone

I could only be grateful
That he had been there

(Rose Hall Warnke)

Mike:

It's really hard to write about yourself — and to remain objective! As regards the preacher-versus-man dichotomy that Rose has initiated, I do want to say that I am both a preacher and a man. Certainly, as preachers go, however, I fear that I fail to fit the mold!

There is another important distinction that must be made: I am also an entertainer — a comedian, if you will — who endeavors to use the vehicle of comedy to convey spiritual truths. This makes me a relatively unique species in the Kingdom of God! (Not particularly special — just unique!)

For many years, I've studied the Scriptures. God's Word is the foundation on which I've built my life and ministry. In the Bible, I've seen my own life reflected. I love the honesty of St. Paul, the loving spirit of John, the humanity of Peter. Those men were not perfect, but God used them.

One of the passages of the Bible that means the most to me is found in First Corinthians:

> Brothers, think of what you were when you were called. Not many of you were wise by human standards; not many were influential; not many were of noble birth. But God chose the foolish things of the world to shame the wise; God chose the weak things of the world to shame the strong. He chose the lowly things of this world and the despised things — and the things that are not — to nullify the things that are, so that no one may boast before him.
>
> (1 Cor. 1:26-29)

Mike Warnke — man, preacher, clown — is one of the foolish things of the world. I am also a weak thing of the world, and lowly. I was not noble born. But, glory be to God, He has seen fit to use me to shame the wise, and to confound the mighty. His strength has been made perfect in my weakness.

As I go through this divorce, God is at work in my life. He assures me of His love for me. He continues to unfold His plan for my life. He is not finished with me. It is that certainty, coming through faith, that enables me to keep on keeping on. Even now, plans are underway for both Rose and me to produce more videos and books. The rigorous schedule of hundreds of concerts a year continues to build, and I stand in amazement and awe at how God is able to use me to help to accomplish His purposes in spite of my weakness, my sin, my dysfunction. It humbles me to realize that He has called me.

Another scripture that gives me great strength during this "passage" in my life was also written by Paul:

I do not understand what I do. For what I want to do I do not do, but what I hate I do. And if I do what I do not want to do, I agree that the law is good. As it is, it is no longer I myself who do it, but it is sin living in me. I know that nothing good lives in me, that is, in my sinful nature. For I have the desire to do what is good, but I cannot carry it out. For what I do is not the good I want to do — this I deep on doing. Now if I do what

I do not want to do, it is no longer I who do it, but it is sin living in me that does it. So I find this law at work: When I want to do good, evil is right there with me. For in my inner being I delight in God's law; but I see another law at work in the members of my body, waging war against the law of my mind and making me a prisoner of the law of sin at work within my members. What a wretched man I am! Who will rescue me from this body of death? Thanks be to God — through Jesus Christ our Lord!

(Rom. 7:15-25)

The Great Apostle also wrote, "But where sin increased, grace increased all the more, so that, just as sin reigned in death, so also grace might reign through righteousness to bring eternal life through Jesus Christ our Lord" (Rom. 5:20-21).

Even when we are not perfect (which is always), God's grace is always there to restore and renew us. We can never deserve or earn so rich a grace. Indeed, we become a debtor to all that God has done for us in Jesus Christ, His Son. He is made perfect in our weakness. His grace is sufficient for us. He truly loves us!

Yes, He even loves the victims of divorce. In fact, He treasures us because He knows we are broken vessels that He can use.

When the great theologian, Karl Barth, was asked what was the greatest truth he had learned in more than

sixty years of study of the Scriptures, he responded
simply: "Jesus loves me, this I know, for the Bible tells
me so."

Another verse of that wonderful chorus presents
even more truth:

> Jesus loves me when I'm good,
> When I do the things I should.
> Jesus loves me when I'm bad,
> But it makes Him, oh, so sad.

As I reflect on our Lord's wonderful love and
grace, I am reminded of another passage from the book
of Romans. It clearly states what I believe about my
own humanity, my sin, and my relationship to the Lord
Jesus Christ:

> What shall we say, then? Shall we go on
> sinning so that grace may increase? By no
> means!...For sin shall not be your master,
> because you are not under law, but under
> grace.   (Rom. 6:1,2,14)

John Newton wrote about that "Amazing Grace"
of God. I identify so strongly with the following verse
from his classic hymn:

> Through many dangers, toils and snares,
> I have already come,
> 'Tis grace hath brought me safe thus far,
> And grace will lead me home.

Sometimes I don't do what I want to do. Those are my sins of omission. Sometimes I do what I don't want to do. Those are my sins of commission. God, in His mercy and grace, has forgiven me of all my sins of omission and commission.

The failure of our marriage resulted in part from both kinds of sins. I omitted to do many things to make my marriage better, and I did many things that made our marriage worse. In short, I failed miserably. But God doesn't see me as a failure. He lovingly extends His forgiveness to me; He offers me a lasting hope. There is a future for the fallen!

The thought of fame makes me uncomfortable. Being seen and recognized is embarrassing for me. Not because I don't like the people who think so much of me, but because I know who I really am. They see me as the person who lives in their minds.

Without the Lord, I'm not much. I remember where I was when He found me, and I know just how long it would take me to sink to that level again if not for Him. To tell the truth, that side beckons to me more than I would like to admit.

"A quick zap and all your problems will vanish in the mist," or "A slight backslide would feel so good right now." There are times when I can hear Satan whisper those words so clearly. I can taste the pleasure of revenge bittersweet in my mouth. The temptation is to swallow hard and roll right into it.

I hurt so badly. I weep too deeply. I hate. I long to give in and not have to fight any more. To rest. To have nothing expected of me. To have no standard to uphold. To be anonymous. And that's just what the devil wants. The best way to win a war is to rob your enemy of his will to fight.

There are times when I think I can't take one more step, face one more problem or disappointment, admit to one more mistake — raise my sword to strike one more blow. But, somehow, through the love of the Lord, I do. So much for the "glamour life," wouldn't you say?

Most people think that the kind of life I lead is just one long party. Getting to travel to new and exotic places. Staying in five-star hotels and eating sumptuous meals. Meeting exciting people and doing wonderful things with them. Kids come up to me all the time and ask, "Brother Mike, how can I get to do what you do?" I tell them to go home and pray for two years and then if they can do anything else, DO IT!

Let's look at a typical road day. The guy that picks us up at the airport can't answer most of the questions I have about this evening's show because he is not the original sponsor. The first guy backed out because something more important came up (the Attilla-the-Hun fest) and this guy picked up the ball only a week ago. We're late due to weather conditions and flight delays, and as we speed toward the Holiday Inn in Moose Jaw, Mississippi, I wonder if I'll have the time to shower before concert time.

When we arrive at the motel, no one has any idea where our reservations are and so the rooms we need are not available due to the Aardvaark Convention in town. The only accommodations available are rooms with couches that convert into beds. We take them. No time left to shower or to eat. A change of clothing and a splash-down are the best I can manage. Hope my after-shave can cover up some of the B.O!

Beep, beep! Outside the door, beep, beep! It's my ride. The van they used to pick us up at the airport has developed brake problems so now we are using his mom's station wagon. However, the air conditioner is on the blink this fine July evening, so we have to leave the windows down. Halfway to the hall, it starts to rain.

We arrive ten minutes late because of the downpour. There is an air conditioning system in the high school gym, but because classes are not in session, it has been turned off for the summer. (The man who has the key that unlocks it has gone fishing in Nova Scotia!)

You can almost cut the humidity with a knife. Sweat begins to trickle down my back even before I make it to the stage and the lights. It's 98 degrees in the gym, but under those lights, it's about 115! My hairspray starts to melt and run into my eyes. The humidity hovers around 90.

When I start to speak, the feedback drowns me out. The sound man is fighting for control, but by the time we gain it, the sound is so low that as I start up again, someone screams, "I can't hear you!" Then everyone begins shouting. We mess with it some more. I ask, "Can you hear me?"

"No!" the crowd shouts back. And I wonder, "Why are they answering me then?"

We finally strike a medium and plunge on. The echo is so bad that those who miss anything should be able to come back tomorrow and hear what they missed because it will still be bouncing around in the rafters somewhere.

I finish sometime close to 9:30. I'm totally worn out. By the time I get out of the hall, it's after 10:00 PM. (Frequently it's later than this if I have an interview to do.) Then it's fifteen minutes to the motel — 10:15 or 10:30. I call room service but they're closed. Domino's delivery is all that's open at this hour in Moose Jaw. I order a pizza with mushrooms and sausage, extra cheese. Thirty minutes later it arrives with two diet Cokes. In the meantime, I call home. Everyone is fine, but sleepy. Good night.

After I eat, I fall asleep with the TV on. And at 6:00 AM it starts all over again. Fifteen to twenty shows a month for the past TWENTY YEARS.... Like I said, if you can do anything else, DO IT!

Every so often, I take a week off. It's nice to be home, but I'm exhausted. Sleeping and eating are about all I can muster the steam to do. The family wants more, but I have nothing left to give. When we first got married, Rose understood, but as things between us progressed from bad to worse, it became quite a bone of contention.

One of the problems seemed to be that I had become acclimatized to the road. That is to say, I spent so much time out that I couldn't relate to what being home meant.

Rose tells stories about me trying to put in wake-up calls from my own bedroom at home. Of my being hungry, and without thinking, picking up the phone to call room service in my own house. She said once that I can't be totally at ease anywhere unless there is that little bar of soap, plain white towels and a paper strap on the toilet seat that reads, "Sanitized for your protection."

There is an old saying, "Absence makes the heart grow fonder." Nothing could be further from the truth. Absence actually makes the heart grow colder. And in learning to deal with loneliness, it's not uncommon for the lonely one to build an entire life that excludes the missing member. This is very true on an emotional level. And with the emotional separation, there is a cooling of intimacy and physical contact. It gets to the place where even a kiss seems to be an invasion of someone else's space.

The bitterness generated by this kind of rejection goes deep. I know. It makes you question everything about yourself. The kind of person you are. The kind of man or woman you are. Your physical looks and sexual attractiveness. If you already have a problem with low self-esteem, what I have just described is almost an invitation to suicide. At least that's how it affected me.

Living with the loss of those things in my relationship with Rose proved to be too much for me. I tried as many ways as I could think of to recapture the feeling, but with my road life being what it is (and was), the time to give it a real shot never seemed to present itself. Once I even tried to come off the road some. I planned to cut things back to just three days a week (Thursday, Friday and Saturday), but by that time, the split was so wide between us that we spent the extra time being at each other's throats. It seemed to me that Rose felt her space had been invaded, and I felt unwanted and totally unneeded. For me, it is, was and always will be a matter of rejection, either real or perceived.

> On the road again. I
> can't wait to get on
> the road again. . . .

One of these days, I'm going to have to confront Willie Nelson!

None of this has anything to do with whether or not I will keep on keeping on with what I do best. I have often said that the only way they will get me to stop is to carry me out, feet first. All I'm trying to say is that this sort of life style has its drawbacks and its costs. To start takes heart. To stay you have to pay. The price differs from person to person, but there is always a price tag. The question is, can you make it without going broke?

The answer depends on whose account you are drawing on. The human bank has its limits. You can only draw so much before you become emotionally, mentally and physically bankrupt. You want to die, quit, hide yourself away. I cannot fully express how I fight against these feelings when I am so tired.

The Lord, on the other hand, has a limitless account. There is no way to draw on Him for more than He has. This "Jesus account" becomes the only place to turn to in times of unabating pain. God is the only place where there is always enough. Your friends may run out of patience. Your spouse may run out of love. Your therapist may run out of answers. But the Lord never runs out on you at all.

I believe that bad things happen because of human failings and shortcomings. That God loves us enough to allow us to make our own decisions. Because we are human, the decisions we make are not always the best. That's where forgiveness and grace come in. The foundations on which flawed men and women have the chance to build new lives. There seems to be no dearth of these two commodities in the heart of Jesus. But in the heart of the Church, compassion can sometimes turn up in very short supply.

I have to put my faith in God, even though I am not perfect. (Especially because I'm not perfect.) I remember a line from an old hymn, "My faith is built on nothing less than Jesus' love and righteousness." My righteousness is as "filthy rags," but His righteousness is not only something I can believe in, but I can count on it as well. It's this faith that keeps me going. It gives me answers to questions that seem to have no answers. It enables me to overcome in spite of myself. For that reason alone, I will never stop serving Him.

Let's Get Real!!

Last night, after the show, the pastor and his wife were taking me back to the hotel. He was driving. As we cruised along at a godly fifty-five, he said to me over his shoulder, "Mike, you travel all over the country. Maybe you can tell me what's going on."

He was referring to the raging warfare going on in the Church, not to spiritual warfare against the enemy, but just "good ol' down and dirty" between the brothers and sisters. I knew just exactly what he meant. It's getting rather brutal out here.

We all know the famous cases. The TV evangelist who lost it all due to an old indiscretion. Caught and hounded by a brother — one who had set himself up as judge and jury. I guess this latter man considered himself to be called of God to "cut out the cancer" that was growing in the Body of Christ. many were amazed to find out later that this "holy surgeon" was himself guilty of the crime he preached against. Still later, we saw this same man taken to court by another minister whom he had ruined. The man suing was guilty by his own admission, but his lawsuit wasn't about the right or wrong of the allegations; instead, it was about the damage that was caused by the truth. If it weren't so sad, it would be almost funny.

"Watch-dogism" has become the sport of choice in much of the Church today. Getting the "low-down" on others and then using that information to destroy them. When there is no "low-down" to get, oftentimes people will make up something out of half-truths and suppositions. Usually the next step in this hideous process is for the victim to be slandered by all and sundry without him ever being approached by the slanderers! When someone does confront the one who is targeted by the slander and the accusations, the identity of the original source of the rumor or the attack is normally withheld. Even if the evidence proves to be true, where is the justice in this approach? Where is the compassion? The grace? The maturity? Where is "restoring a brother in love"? And, yes, where is Jesus?

Recently, a pastor friend of mine was kicked out of his church. He was relieved of his pulpit by his district superintendent during the Sunday worship service in front of his entire congregation and his family with no warning whatsoever. He came prepared to preach; he left in disgrace. His sin? He had increased the number of black families in an otherwise upper-middle-class, white church, and a few of the "money people" didn't like it!

Of course, they couldn't simply say, "We're a bunch of bigoted jerks!" so the charge was "he changed the traditional make-up of the church body by introducing into it elements hitherto not present." So the pastor and his family are gone now, and so are many members of the congregation who couldn't stomach this kind of hypocrisy. The "money people" got what they wanted. The district superintendent got what he wanted. The only persons who didn't get what they wanted were my friend and the Lord. The pastor loved to serve that church. God had called him to do exactly that. But, because of envy, pride and racial prejudice, Satan got what he wanted too!

A beloved contemporary Christian artist has recently had the good fortune to have been able to cross over with her music to the secular world. Both her songs and her videos are doing well. Has the Church jumped to its feet to offer encouragement and support?

Not on your sacred calf! Frequently, I hear comments like: "She's sold out!" Wouldn't it be better to say, "She's made a breakthrough!" We should be acknowledging her success instead of saying, "She's a traitor!" It would be more appropriate to say, "She's a soldier who is right-smack-dab in the middle of the enemy's camp!"

Someone remarked, "But her music doesn't sound the same as it did when she was fifteen!"

Of course it doesn't! She grew up. She's no longer a little girl, shy and frightened. She's a grown woman with her own family and the courage to do what a lot of people only dream of doing. There is one other thing she has too: a heart for Jesus.

Just because Jesus isn't mentioned in every line of a song (if at all) doesn't mean He isn't included. Even if the song is about something as tawdry as human love, commitment and caring.

Human love is viewed by most people as "nasty." I'm of the opinion that most folks who think this way do so because they view human love the same way the world does. The god of this world (Satan) has taken something that the Lord intended for the good of His people and twisted it out of all recognition. And what baffles me is that the majority of people in the Church seem to have bought this line. No wonder that singing about human emotions seems vile to such people. In their minds it is. But whose fault is that? It's not the Lord's and it's certainly not His servant's.

Whatever happened to "Be kind to one another, tender-hearted, forgiving one another"? Do we really have to find fault with our brothers and sisters to make the Body of Christ a fit place to be? Are we called to hunt witches or are we called to preach Jesus? Aren't we called to preach Him crucified and risen from the dead? Does the Lord need a "Gospel gestapo" to get His will accomplished in the lives of those He's called into His service? I don't think so. No one is really called to mind everyone's business but their own.

There seems to be so many reasons these days to turn our backs on each other. Distractions come in the form of offenses — the real, imagined or just plain fabricated. I am hard-pressed to understand how any of this glorifies God or adds to Him Kingdom in any way. Not only is it hurtful within the Body of Christ itself, but the witness it presents to the secular world is totally scandalous. Far from seeing us as people whose actions are geared to upholding a godly standard of holiness, much of the world views us as a bunch of self-righteous, narrow-minded, hard cases with no love, mercy or understanding for anyone, including ourselves! And, in many cases, we would find it very difficult to prove them wrong. Most people go by what they see, not what they hear. We can preach the love of Jesus till "hell freezes over," but until we are willing to live the life of love in a daily, practical way, we are simply "howling at the moon."

I have no doubt that Rose and I will be attacked good and proper for the decisions and mistakes we have made. Some people will want us to answer their questions about every intimate detail of our life together. There will be those who will want me to dish up some dirt on Rose so that I can come out of this looking like the good guy. Still others will want her to do the same. It's like sharks going into a feeding frenzy. When "the keepers of all that is sacred" smell blood, they run to get in on the kill. The truly scary thing is how good these Pharisees feel after the massacre is over.

Anyhow, I have no dirt to dish on Rose. Even if I did, I wouldn't. What's the point? I remember that story in the Bible about Nehemiah rebuilding the walls of Jerusalem. The work was going well, but the leaders of the nations nearby felt very insecure. To them, the new wall meant the leaders sent emissaries to invite Nehemiah to a conference at which he would have a change to explain himself. The plan was to kill God's servant at this meeting. They had no real wish to understand, only a desire to remove that which they believed to be a threat. I often think of Nehemiah's reply to those who were sent to deceive him. "I am doing a mighty work. I have no time to come down to you." In other words, Nehemiah was not about to abandon God's work in order to debate an absurd accusation made by a bunch of folks who were in no position to know the truth or weren't even real about their desire to hear it.

As you already know, many things went wrong between Rose and me. A lot of those problems were there, in our lives, long before we met each other. Emotional land mines were hidden beneath the surface, and we weren't aware of them until we were blown sky-high! The process we have been through to keep our ministry and friendship in one piece has been a long and painful one. There were a lot of times when I felt like just throwing my hands up and forgetting about it. But I didn't. Rose most probably felt the same way, and she didn't give up either. I think there should be some recognition of what we've accomplished rather than only scorn for how we have messed up. Some love, prayer and support rather than a spade of dirt in the face.

I remember once hearing a very well-known atheist say that she had no desire to join the army of God because it was the only army in the history of man that killed it's own wounded as a matter of policy!

There are many people, called of God, who no longer minister in His name because when they needed someone to be there for them, no one came. And the ones who did come were there only to kill! I don't know what happened in Sam Kennison's life, for example, but it must have been horrible. Sam is a very well-known secular comedian who makes a point of letting everyone know that he was once a preacher. He now drives a Corvette with a license place that reads, "EX-REV."

Whereas once Sam had proclaimed the Gospel, he now seems to go out of his way to appear lewd, crude and sacrilegious. I heard one of his tapes. He is an excellent comedian. The fire and energy he once used to preach God's Word is now in the enemy's hands. How that must hurt the heart of God.

I refuse to be driven away! If God wants to take me to another place, that's a whole different deal. I will submit to that without any reservations. But I will not give up what I am doing just because there are those who do not agree with the way I conduct my personal life. Neither will I defer to those who think that because I'm not perfect I have nothing to say about Jesus.

So I messed up. Does that change who Jesus is? Does it alter the fact that God sent His Son to redeem us and he sent His Spirit to guide us? If I were telling people to accept me, to turn their lives over to Mike Warnke, it would be a different matter. If I were preaching myself rather than Christ, then there really would be a problem. The fact is, however, I've never pushed anything but Jesus. I have never said, "be like me." I've always preached, "Find God's will for your life and do your best to do it." That's true even if events in my life reveal my own struggle to do that very thing! There have been victories and there have been failures. At the very least, I'm trying to be up-front about it, and so is Rose.

One group is after me even as I type these words. They have been trying to find something that will discredit me for some time now. They run a magazine and from what I hear they want to trash one of my books *(The Satan Seller)* by somehow "proving" that what I wrote never really happened. To accomplish this goal, they have called old friends, family members and even some old enemies of mine to see what they can dig up. Never once have they come to me.

As a matter of fact, one of my friends asked why I hadn't been contacted, and they replied, "We have his story in the book. We don't want to hear any more from him." I wouldn't even know about what's going on if it weren't for the fact that most of the people they have contacted have called to let me know. I guess the plan was to trash me in print without me ever finding out it was coming. That's called blind-siding; It's against the rules in football, but not, I guess, in the Body of Christ. What do I plan to do about this? Nothing. Just think of Nehemiah and his wall, I guess. Pray for those who despitefully use me? That's a good idea. Where did I hear that? Oh, yeah!

There is so much to do and things are going so fast that I often feel that one minute wasted is a life lost!

Inasmuch as I have given my life over to helping save others, I have no deep need to involve myself in anything that will keep me from that goal. If that's the sort of party you'd invite me to, I'm sorry, you'll just have to dance with someone else! Better yet, learn to dance alone!

Editor:

One of the most hopeful messages of this book is contained within this chapter. Mike and Rose Warnke are able to remain friends even after their divorce. They are able to see each other's strengths as well as their weaknesses. God has given them the ability to look at each other with a measure of objectivity. As both have pointed out so vividly, this is the grace of God at work in their lives.

It is clear that their Christian commitment pervades every part of their lives. They are able to share God's love together even though they may not like certain things about each other.

I love Rose's very human description of Mike. There's such hope and assurance derived from seeing his humanity. The Body of Christ needs more of this kind of transparency in order for our fellowship to become real. Too often we're afraid to reveal our real selves to one another because of the negative judgments such revelations could engender.

How can the Church become the healing body it is designed to be if its members continue to hide behind masks that cover the realities of who we are?

Many books are being written concerning this issue. Christians, like the rest of humanity, have many areas that need healing and love in their lives. Christians need to experience recovery from hurts and rejection too.

Those who are involved in public ministry are often the most hidden of all. Because so many have placed them on such high pedestals, it is frequently impossible to see them as being simply human. Possibly this is why so many Christian leaders have fallen; they felt unable to reveal their humanity to others for fear of rejection and loss of status.

We are called upon to support our leaders in more ways than one: through prayer, encouragement, love and financial commitments. We can let them know that we will be there for them no matter what problems they face. That, in the final analysis, is the meaning of commitment after all.

The warm sense of humor, the ability to laugh that have carried Rose and Mike through some difficult times is very healthy indeed. Without taking themselves too seriously, they are able to laugh at each other's foibles and mistakes.

This is possible because they recognize their humanity. As someone once said, "To err is human; I'm uncomfortable around *gods*."

Let us pray for Mike and Rose as they, in their humanity, seek to fulfill the commission God has called them to accomplish.

10

The Priority of Love — a Lasting Friendship

Love delights in giving attention rather
    than in attracting it.
Love finds the element of good and builds
    on it.
Love does not magnify defects.
Love is a flame that warms but never
burns.
Love knows how to disagree without
becoming
    disagreeable.
Love rejoices at the success of others
instead
    of being envious.

(Father James Keller)

Rose:

November, 1989

I pulled away from him slowly
Like a bandage off a healing wound.
One by one
I could feel the circuits break,
Slowly disconnecting us
Like a slow motion

The hands I once loved
Became unfamiliar to me.
Today
A person I once hid against
From the world — has
Become invisible...

It took hours
To travel from the kitchen
To the back door
Where I stepped through to find hope.

There were pieces of him
Stuck to me
All over.

I knew if I could just pass
Through that door
I could cry
Alone.

On the porch overlooking the lake
And inside
Eight miles away
I could scream
Until it was safe
To go back to the world —

One by one
I watched the notes go out of tune
And all the love in the world
Changed.

He won't be home, after all. Home was just
    Another word for us,
And the only us I knew

Was in a photograph
That someone had taken
　　Only if they had known.....

Would it have made a difference?
Sometimes I think it might have
Then I realize...; we made our
　　course!
　　　　Somehow
　　　　　　with help we didn't even know about
　　　　　　　　(Rose Hall Warnke)

There Was a Time

He's away from me now.
　　Not in time
　　　　But in space.
And yes, there were times
　　I was lonesome,
But not for him,
　　　　Only for the way I wanted him
　　　　To make me feel.

I wonder if eyes have a memory
　　As well as the mind?

I can't remember what he felt like anymore,
　　Only the way I felt
　　When he looked at me....

There was a time
When I loved him so much

Just the air he was angry in
        Would hurt me.
It was frightening
To need someone
        That violently...

And, there was a time
It was more frightening...not
        To feel that way
                Anymore.
                        (Rose Hall Warnke)

CAN WE BE FRIENDS — AFTER WE COULDN'T OR WOULDN'T BE MARRIED?

This will be the final writing I will do on this book of hope and recovery! And how appropriate it is to complete it in this manner.

There is a privilege in being someone's.....anyone's.....friend. Friendship is a remarkable gift we often take for granted. And then, to have someone who wants you to be his or her friend....this too carries an even greater weight of responsibility.

But before we go into how two people can even consider being friends after they couldn't be married, let's talk about how difficult it is to understand and love ourselves, and each other. All of us born — all of us will die — some of us will live and some of us will only exist in life. Some of us will laugh and dance and some will sit and cry, and some will do both. And some of us will meet someone we feel we want to spend the rest of our lives with, and we decide to marry that person.

Then there will be some of us who, for whatever or how many reasons, will not succeed in that marriage. Then, some of us will die. . . . some of us will live and some of us will only exist in life.

"Learning"
One the Same

You learned my name
You learned my ways
They became your own.
And when you reacted to me
You reacted to yourself.

Hands of the same person
Must learn
To greet one another.
We were together so long
We became one another,

Yet————
I felt you wore me as a coat
I covered you————protected you

And then you took me off
Laid me on the edge of a chair
Of your life
And walked away
Saying something about
Turning a corner—————

I do not know about corners
I wonder
If I will learn------
(Rose Hall Warnke)

Then, some of us will sit and cry and some of us will laugh and dance, and some of us, will do both.

It will be our choice....a difficult choice, but, a choice.

There are choices in life.

They are difficult....they are easy. However they are, they must be made. What would your choice be in your difficult situation?

I have been faced with many decisions in my life. Never, however, have I been faced with one as difficult as this.

I know you are thinking I am talking about this divorce....

No, I am not. And our decision to divorce was not easy. Especially when you believe you are going against what you want, what you believe, what you feel you need.

No, the choice I am talking about is the decision and choice to be Michael's friend. And not just his friend in words. His true friend. In deed and words and work!

Older

There are some things I meant
To say to you when we were old

Perhaps because I always really thought
We would grow old---together!

You were always so much more important
To me than any work I did of my own

And I always wanted to be more secure
In being your lady than anything I ever did.

Getting older makes it easier to define,
To speak of matters of the heart

Getting older makes it easier to
Get older----

(Rose Hall Warnke)

Ironic, isn't it? That it would be easier to be Michael's friend than to have been his wife.

It is coming winter now. The leaves are mostly brown, some that are left are yellow and a few are red. It is 55 degrees today, overcast, misty rain, very cold looking — yet so comfortable. . . .

The farm is full of all those fallen leaves lying on the ground around all those old majestic trees. The wind is blowing furiously. The leaves that are still on the trees are turning loose of their last chance to FEEL life as they know it. To know life only for one season.

How like the trees and leaves we are. And yet, there is a difference.

Michael and I were two individuals when we met. We were relatively young in years, yet very strong, very weak and very worn in our hearts and in our heads. In both our lives, life had dealt severely with us in very different ways.

We attempted to combine our lives in what we humans call marriage. We attempted to become one tree.

Home

There's a house
  Somewhere on a farm
    It's quiet now.
But once in 1990, in June,
It was full of people
  Moving boxes of things
    To somewhere else

I didn't see you then as going,
  Only as passing through.
Somehow you never left
  But you are gone now———

I think I understand how it feels
  To not know about home
When you never had one
  To show you

Even though we moved to the farm in 1983,
  You never really
    lived there

How is it that now
  That you're gone,
I can now live here?
Is it because it's all I have left of you?
I wish I had known about home before.
I am grateful to know now———
                    (Rose Hall Warnke)

   This was what I believed was how it "should" be. And so did Michael.

   It was not possible.....

   Now we have been given the opportunity, the gift, perhaps even the commission to continue to be friends. I do not yet know fully what it all means.

   What I do know is that the Lord does not want my heart to break and become bitter....or, for my mouth to speak in such a way that I would harm myself, or you...or my family....or for my mouth to speak in doubt or dishonor of Him....

   What I do know is that the Lord does not want my life or my service to Him or Michael's life or his service to Him to end.....

   What I do know is that Jesus would have me to be an example of Him. And what better opportunity to attempt to be that than in this place of difficult transition and change.

Reasons Disguised

It is not always the absence of love
That makes me feel alone.
Often it's been too much love
  Given to me by people
  For the wrong reasons
  That keeps me here, alone.
Gladly — rather than have life sucked
Out of me by violent needs
  Of other minds.

I am ungrateful
  I am sad
Not to have had arms put around me
And give me something more
Than polite manipulations

  Oh, how I tried
  I think they should know how
    I tried
To pretend I didn't notice————

Now I choose———I choose to
  Be alone
Rather than wrapped in arms
  I never needed—————
                    (Rose Hall Warnke)

You see, I have not stopped loving Michael. I have changed the kind of love I have for him. I have not stopped wanting to give to Michael. I have changed some of the ways I can give to him. I have not stopped believing Michael needs me. I have not stopped believing *in* Michael.

I have set aside our differences and failures and focused on our qualities and strengths as individuals.

What I have done is to realize more of what and who Michael is to me. What I have done is to decide!

What I have decided and I know is that I am to be his friend after I couldn't be his wife. . . .

There is a family of four in a little white house on a hill. I have only been inside the house two times.

There is a man there. There is a woman. There are two children. One is a little girl about eight years old. The other is a little boy around four years old.

The little girl is beautiful. She goes to school. The little boy is beautiful too. He is unable to walk, unable to sit, to feed himself, to talk, to see. He lives with the effects of the streptococcus he was stricken with at birth that was followed by meningitis.

He smiles all the time.

His mother is very tiny, about five feet tall. She weighs ninety pounds. She holds the little boy a lot. She plays with the little girl. Often the man and the little girl are together at the pond below their house, fishing. They have cats and dogs. Their blue jeans and sheets hang on the clothes line outside. They have a washer and dryer too.

Their house is full of treasures they have collected and hung on the walls. Pictures of everyone are displayed throughout the house. Toys and stuffed animals and wonderful things children love are bulging the children's room. They share the same room. The house is very small and it is a wonderfully kept home.

They have lived there for three years. They rent the house. I am certain they do not get along sometimes. Not because I know this, but just because they are human beings.

The man and the woman lead a simple life. They take care of themselves, and do not bother anyone else. I do not know if they are married. "Talk" is that they are not. I wonder how folks would know about that?

We all know about folks who "talk" though, don't we?

I wonder if anyone knows about the tender little boy. Or about the woman's devotion to him. I wonder if anyone knows about the beautiful little girl. Or about how much time the man spends with her every summer day walking in the fields and fishing at the pond.

I wonder if anyone knows about the care the woman takes of the man or the time and care the man takes of the woman.

I wonder if anyone even cares to know? The only "talk" I have ever heard is whether or not they are married.

I wonder?

Did anyone take the time to find out if they are married? Did anyone tell them about Jesus and the importance of Christian marriage? Or did people simply talk?

Sometimes things are not what they seem. And sometimes they are more than they seem. I'm talking about evil and good.

And sometimes we are asked to make a choice. Not just in what we think, but in how we are going to behave. Too much of the time we think and talk one way, and we behave another. That goes along with being human too.

And there are times when we *know* we have to stand for what we know to be good and right and Christ-like! Even if it isn't usual, or common, or "normally" acceptable, or, what everyone thinks we *should* do: and sometimes even when we don't know how to do any of it.

I am not the only person to ever be the wife of a Christian leader or to be a Christian leader who has experienced the horrible death of divorce. In fact, I am one in 60 percent of all married couples who divorce. Somehow this should be some comfort. *It is not!*

Realizing I have failed and knowing how many others have failed along with me does not comfort me. Neither does it justify me.

Still, do you think it is possible to get into the "lifeboat of Jesus" in the midst of the massive raging river of destruction of divorce?

Do you think it is possible to recover from the rubble of divorce a deeper sense of awareness of what life and Jesus are all about?

Can I as a human failure from the "outrageous downfall" of my marriage redeem more than a fragment of what I know His love wants for me?

Do you think? Is it possible?

For seventeen years I have served a loving, wondrous God. Through His Word and in my own living journey. I have searched furiously for the meaning to life — for the answers to man's dilemmas.

I think I live in enemy territory, as well as in the safe haven of His arms. Every new day I face is a challenge and it is also an opportunity.

And I know, without a moment's hesitation, "Faith is being sure of what we hope for and certain of what we do not see" even when I fall!

When God told Joshua to take the land of Canaan from the enemies of God, God's word to Joshua was: "Be strong and courageous, do not be terrified; do not be discouraged, for the Lord your God will be with you wherever you go."

I am a human being! I can be discouraged or terrified. And as a human, when I am discouraged or terrified, it is proper to allow myself that human time.....IT JUST ISN'T OKAY TO STAY *IN* THAT TIME.

You see, God didn't say, "Rose, you won't feel terrified or discouraged." He said, "BE STRONG." He said that He doesn't *want me* to be terrified or discouraged. And what loving parent would ever want their children to be fearful and weak? And yet, He knows there will be those fearful, weak times, those circumstances, for all of us, and He said, "FOR THE

LORD YOUR GOD WILL BE WITH YOU WHEREVER YOU GO."

I wish I could say I had been an excellent wife. I can't. I was not an excellent wife. I wish I could say I have been an excellent mother. I cannot say that either. There are many different criteria, requiring different skills for being different things to different people.

What I can say, though, is that I do the best I know how!

What I can say is that I try.

What I can say is that I have been an excellent friend, business partner, and manager. And now, I have the challenge, and the opportunity, to continue to be that friend. Can I be an excellent friend? Yes!!!

How do I know? Because I have already been able to be an excellent friend. Not only to Michael, but to my children and others as well.

And in the aftermath of this divorce, I have the most challenging and greatest opportunity to fulfill what I know I am able to do.

So, you see, this part may be easier.....

And in doing so, I pray you will experience with me the necessity to come from this (our) divorce with us not as enemies in destruction, but friends in Christ in support of each other, and in support of a calling of God on both our lives. A calling much greater than the humanness we feel in our failures.

A calling to be in His image. . . . A calling to love Him with all our hearts, minds and souls. . . . A calling

to love each other....and you....and finally a calling
to love ourselves as well.....

Investment

Moments once unpredictable
  Have become easily predictable
It is safe to say they will
  Stay the same — even if they change---

There was a period they
  Crumbled liked crackers---

How did we get to where we are?
  Our investment was so great

The time---the love---the heart
  It must return something!

It is time to observe---take watch
  Be patient

We are staying the same, Yet
  We are changing---

(Rose Hall Warnke)

Can you imagine the results if we can all learn and
strive to love through pain?

Can you dream big enough to believe that, with
the direction of our glorious Jesus, this is possible?

How do we know unless we try? Will you go with
me on this opportunity?

Or will you make it more difficult by accusing, blaming, criticizing, and falling victim to Satan's way of condemning?

This is not a safe place to walk. A place where you defy traditions, and live the Word.....BUT IT IS A VICTORIOUS PLACE TO WALK!

AND. IT IS THE TIME.....TIME TO SEE GOD'S PLANS FOR HIS CHILDREN INSTEAD OF US LIVING OUR PLANS FOR GOD.

I look forward to HIS sufficient grace as He demonstrates His power in the midst of all my failure, all my thorns, all my weakness.

I look forward to continuing to serve Him even fuller and greater than I have already been allowed....I look forward to loving Him and you and myself....even more than I already have or feel worthy to.....My hope and my confidence is in Him!

I look forward to continuing to be and to becoming an even better friend to Michael.

Mike:

We're hearing the word "priorities" all the time these days. I guess, to be truthful, I've heard about priorities all my life. Most of the time the topic's been mentioned to me in passing or in theory. You know what I mean. Someone would begin to complain about not having enough time for this or that. A once-important part of this or that person's life had fallen by the wayside. Perhaps it was a forgotten relative or a misplaced friend. Those taking part in the discussion would sagely nod their heads and say, "Yeah, man, ya gotta have priorities."

The idea behind priorities is to pick those things that are most important in your life and to give them first place. To devote time and energy to them before you waste too much of either on things that are really of no consequence or of lesser consequence. In so doing, you are able to insure, to a very large extent, the success of both business and personal endeavors. Also, by prioritizing, time can be budgeted and it won't be able to slip by unnoticed.

I have six children, but I have been to only one graduation. I have missed any number of birthdays and other special occasions. I was in attendance for the birth of my first granddaughter (barely), but missed the birth of the second. Why? I was on the road. I was convinced that my service to God was in traveling for Him, and I'm sure it is. I no longer feel, however, that the Lord calls me to do this to the detriment of my family.

My kids have grown up, in large part, without me. This is most true of my sons who were raised by their mother as products of a previous failed marriage. It's a sad thing to look up one day and find yourself surrounded by grown men and women, and you can't seem to remember seeing your small children grow up. My children have experienced many problems stemming from my lack of availability to them. To some extent, they still do. We are working on it. There is no way I can even express how this makes me feel. My son Brendon once told me he hated God for taking me away from him. My God, what have I done?

It's too bad that some of us don't figure out early in life what is important. When we're young, the whole idea seems to be to live up to the "American dream." This is especially true for men. We are taught from a very young age that success, position and financial achievement are the things that define what a man is. The pressure to make grades, go to college to "make something out of your life," are familiar themes in many American homes. This injunction to do well is often followed by talk that makes it clear that no one really expects you to do so.

In my early life, I was repeatedly told that I wouldn't amount to anything. After all, I was the by-product of two drunks who weren't even married at the time of my conception. My parents were married before I was born, but, apparently, not by much. From almost the beginning, I have felt a real need to prove all of "them" wrong. I have pushed myself to the point of sickness many times just to prove that I could do what people said I couldn't. A lot of what has kept me on the road all these years is tied up in these feelings.

I remember when I first came to my record company about fifteen years ago. There was a person in control of much of what I did who had no faith in me at all. The only reason I was even considered for a recording contract was because my friends Nancy Honeytree Miller and Paul Paino, Jr. went to bat for me. I heard comments from the person who was the head of my division at that time that indicated that he felt I was a fluke or a freak and I would never stand the test of time. Other things that were said made me soon realize that the powers that be felt that "talk" albums would not sell, and that what I did was a total waste of time and money. I also learned that my contact at the company hated to do photo shots of me for cover art because he considered me to be too ugly to photograph well. This was a lot to overcome for someone as green as I was.

I want to hasten to add, however, that the situation I've described no longer exists. That guy is gone. As a matter of fact, I have seen a lot of people come and go at the company. Today, I count among some of my best friends and most ardent supporters the staff and management of my recording company, Word, Inc. (I want to take this opportunity to express special thanks for the good years to Roland Lundy, Tom Ramsey and to my special friend, Lynn Keesecker. There are three others who are no longer with Word but were when it mattered, whose help I would also like to acknowledge: Neal Joseph, Barry Lanids and Stan Mosier.

I have always had a fear of being a failure. I think this fear is linked to the deeper issue of rejection. It had long been my belief that if I did well, those around me would have a reason to give me the love and acceptance I longed for. I didn't believe anyone could just love me for myself because I was sure that there was nothing personally lovable about me.

The result has been that I've worked my head off to get people to like me. I have served God, yes. But the cost has been so great. I'm not sure the Lord had all of this in mind. Not that He hasn't led me; He has, I know He has. It's just that a lot of *me* has gotten in the way. I've run ahead of the Lord out of impatience.

I've gotten in His way out of pride. I've taken wrong turns out of stubbornness. I've done ten when He asked for only a four, and that has come from my drive to "be somebody," and because of my fear that I never would be. He has blessed many people through all of this. But it hasn't been because of me; it has been in spite of me. Mostly, I've just been along for the ride.

For years, I've talked about slowing down. I've even made plans for this. But, somehow, when the opportunity comes, there is always a reason to delay and I always take it. "Just one more year and then we can slow down. We can take a little time. We can rest and have time for the family."

In June of 1992 I will mark my twentieth year in full-time ministry. TWENTY YEARS. That's a long time to make a promise you never keep. The reasons are all excellent; the results, unfortunately, aren't the same. I have children who don't know me nearly as well as they have a right to. I have an ex-wife who, thank God, is still a friend at least. And I have a forty-five-year-old body with seventy-five years worth of mileage on it. One hundred and ninety to 200 shows a year. An average of 285,000 air miles a year. What's wrong with this picture?

When you figure all this out after the damage has been done (as most of us do) the only thing you can do is play the cards you've dealt yourself. You learn as much as you can from your mistakes and go on. That's what I'm attempting to do. The work goes on. I hope with a little more attention paid to the voice of the Lord, and a little less to the fears and pressures of the past. Now I pray with a view to priorities as well as possibilities. My lack of understanding has cost a lot. But the Lord is still my God and His grace is still sufficient for all my needs.

I do a lot of writing while I fly (not on my own, but by airplane). We are, just now, landing at the airport in Bismark, North Dakota. The flight attendant is making the usual announcements about tray tables and seat backs and the stuff that we have "stowed" in the overhead compartments.

The F.A.A. has these very strict rules governing where you can put your stuff. It can go either in the overhead compartment or under the seat in front of you. As the space under the seat wouldn't hold a sock box, and if it did there would be no place to put your feet except behind your neck, the overhead gets quite a work-out. In the compartment above you, the contents tend to shift during the flight. Stuff that was well-stowed on take-off can move and become dangerous by the time you land. Things that you were sure were securely stored can fall out of the overhead compartment and knock your brains out!

I'm big on analogy. As I was sitting here listening to the announcements, it dawned on me that the situation I've just described draws a rather nice parallel to what I've been trying to say in this chapter.

When you start out in life, in a relationship or a business venture, you figure you have things stowed to stay put. Everything is exactly where it needs to be according to the regulations. No problem. But then, one day, you open that overhead and find out that due to turbulence in the flight of life, everything has shifted.

Then, when you finally take a peek, it knocks your brains out!

I have this friend who always says, "Life is hard to do." He's right. None of us is going to get out of this life alive. The best we can do is the best we can do.

Now I understand that it is important to try and remember to make frequent checks on the old priorities overhead so the stuff you stow doesn't shift and cave in your life just because you didn't heed the warning to be careful and pay attention. We will all be on board for the final approach one of these days, but there is no reason to let life make you brain-dead in the meantime. And if you do get conked on the noggin once in a while, the only remedy is to learn the lesson and keep on going. It's just like riding a horse. If the sucker bucks you off, get up and get back on. If you don't, you'll never ride again.

Yes, I've learned a lot about what is really important during the past few years. There are some things I can fix and some that I can't. There is nothing that I can undo. The guilt is the thing that is labor with the most. At the same time, however, I know that God doesn't want me to feel guilty. God wants me to feel conviction. Guilt brings death, but conviction brings change — even to an old dog that's a bit frightened by new tricks.

I'm a great fan of a monk named Thomas Merton. He lived and worked in a monastery called Gethsemani. The abbey is located near my home in central Kentucky. One of the things I love to do most is to spend a day praying and getting refreshed with the monks who live there.

On my way to and from the monastery, I like to listen to some teaching tapes by Thomas Merton. I have also read several of his books (he wrote about sixty during his lifetime). Many books and articles have been written about him. Needless to say, I am also a voracious reader of books by and about Thomas Merton.

He died in the late sixties as the result of a freak accident that occurred when he was in Southeast Asia. I regret that I never had the opportunity to meet him, but his written legacy has drawn me closer in my walk with Jesus than the writings or sayings of any other Christian author (with the exception of the New Testament, of course).

One of his tapes is entitled "Pure Love." It presents a lecture by Merton that was given to the young men studying to become Trappist monks when he was a novice master at the abbey.

As I conclude this chapter on priorities, I want to stress two that are very important to me in this stage of my life: prayer and love. You will find that these two components of the Christian life will do more for you than anything I can think of. They will speed your recovery process even as they are helping me with mine.

Thomas Merton outlined three kinds of love one can have for God:

1. To love Him because He is powerful.
2. To love Him because He is good to us.
3. To love Him simply because He's good.

I'd like to take a few moments now to discuss my perceptions related to these three kinds of love for God. To love Him because He is powerful is the sort of love a slave has for his master. Its motive is to keep the slave out of trouble. It is really a false love that is motivated by fear. It is not able to set the lover free.

Secondly, we can love God because He's good to us. This, as Merton pointed out, is the sort of love a mercenary or an employee has for the person who pays him. It is based on desire, and it can be counted on only as long as the object of the love is fulfilling the lover's desire.

This kind of love cannot set the lover free either because the lover is ruled by his or her desires and wants. This makes it hard for the lover to distinguish the difference between right and wrong, good and bad. It often leads to jealousy, greed, lust, etc.

The third kind of love is the best. This is described as loving God simply because He's good. It's this kind of love that a son has for his father. It's pure love. Such love exists because of the need to love. There is no reason, no thought of gain, no fear with this kind of unconditional love. This kind of love is given just because it's impossible to know the object of the love without loving it. It leads the lover to know God for who He really is. It is the realization that He deserves to be loved just because He is God.

This is the kind of love that sets people free. When you love God like this, you are free to love everyone else because the roof and foundation of that love are immoveable. You are also free to love yourself. This love is not swayed by desire or threatened by fear.

I have learned that a man or woman's life is governed by the way in which he or she loves. Pure love is never partial. It is the work of the Holy Spirit. It is the consummation of the law of God.

Please take the time to read First Corinthians 13. Then turn to 1 John 4. Read both chapters. Don't think of love out of fear (slave love) or love out of desire (mercenary love) but think of the pure love the Father has for you. Then seek the help of the Holy Spirit within you to enable you to begin to yield to loving that way yourself. It will be a giant step in learning to live free.

I know that God loves me with an everlasting love. I know that He loves you. The priority of love in my life is what enables me to love myself. As a result, I am now able to love Rose as my sister in the Lord, and to love all the people I have the privilege to minister to. That love enables us to continue to work together in the service of the King of love.

"God is love. Whoever lives in love lives in God, and God in him. . . . There is no fear in love. But perfect love drives out fear. . . . We love because he first loved us. . . And he has given us this command: Whoever loves God must also love his brother" (1 John 4:16, 18, 19, 21).

God loves you!

Editor:

I had the privilege to go with Mike to the Abbey of Gethsemani near Bardstown, Kentucky, on one beautiful spring afternoon. That trip gave me a glimpse into Mike's heart that I will never forget. We spent a long time in the monastery chapel in silent prayer. God was very close to us. As we got up to leave, I noticed tears in Mike's eyes and I knew that God had been revealing more to my friend about His love for His servant.

Similarly, I have spent many hours with Rose. We have prayed together and shared our hearts and burdens with each other. Her caring and her openness create an atmosphere in which personal growth occurs.

As a result of the time I have spent with both of these servants of God, I have appreciated several things about them. I know they love God and they love to spend time with Him.

I am convinced that it is because of their ongoing relationship with the Father that they are now able to commit themselves to a continuing relationship with each other in ministry. As we have already pointed out, that relationship will take a slightly different form, but many of the roles will remain the same.

The miraculous grace of God is at work in both of their lives. What a testimony it is to the power and love of God to see two formerly married individuals working together in ministry. What a message of hope and victory this gives to the world.

I've learned something else about Mike and Rose as well. They do know how to reach out to people who are in pain. Their own experience with abuse, hardship, brokenness, divorce and fear helps them to understand the needs of the broken-hearted. Their hearts are truly broken with the things that break the heart of God.

What's more, they love to minister to others. They really love people. They care.

All of us can learn much from their experiences. This book shows the road to recovery to all who have fallen and all who have been victimized. I will ever be grateful to Mike and Rose for their courage and honesty in revealing their struggles to us.

They want you to experience the hope that they have found in God. They want you to know His love.

11
Live Your Life as Your Gift to God

by John Joy

If you haven't already done so, please read the introduction to this book in which I explain my role as counselor to Mike and Rose.

In this chapter I'll be talking about marriage and divorce, our ongoing quest for community, freedom, and spiritual integrity. I'll also discuss briefly the role that psychotherapy may play in this ongoing quest.

The Scriptures indicate that we human beings were created on the sixth day of creation. It was the last day of active creation. And we were the last of the last to boot. It's an understatement to say that a lot went on before we got here. A lot that we still know very little about.

Besides being latecomers to the creation drama, the Scriptures also tell us that we are created in God's image: male and female. Though we are fairly frail, dependent creatures, there is something sacred about being a human being. In some fashion, our deepest identities reflect our Creator. In spite of our frailties and limitations, in some mysterious way, the divine radiates in and through our lives.

The quest for personal identity is rooted in our creation in God's image. The sky doesn't search for authentic existence, nor does the sea. Plants don't seek to discover their true identities, nor do the sun, the moon, or the stars. The birds and fish don't ponder the meaning of their existence, nor do our fellow mammals, as far as we know. Only us. Only human beings have a notion that life has some sort of meaning. Only humans quest to discover the ultimate reality within. Only we lay claim to the glory of being created in the image of God.

Yet, should we be tempted to be grandiose in our conceptions, we need only to ponder the evening sky. As astronomers tell us, there are as many stars around as there are grains of sand on the beaches of this earth. Our lives, as important and all-consuming as they often are to us in the big picture, are no more than a grain of sand....on a grain of sand....on a grain of sand....in a boundless and ever-expanding universe.

Thank you for indulging me. I just thought it would be helpful for all of us to put the matters at hand in an appropriate context. Each of us — including Mike and Rose — is one person out of five billion living on planet Earth. We were created in God's image, but we are far from being gods ourselves. We are His creatures.

With that preface in mind, let's look specifically at the pilgrimages of Mike and Rose. As you know, Mike and Rose were legally married. Now they are legally divorced. Mike and Rose are still human beings; they are still created in the image of God. They are still continuing their quest for creative community, freedom, and spiritual integrity. God still loves them.

The Scriptures call us to believe that in some fashion, our marriages are meant to symbolize and enact God's commitment to us. God speaks of himself as the husband; and He calls Israel His wayward bride. Jesus is the groom; the Church is His bride. We men of the cross are to love and serve our women as Christ loved and served His Church.

Women of the cross are to respect and spiritually nourish their chosen men. We are to represent Christ to each other, for each other, and by our love, we are to nurture and care for our mates. This is the spiritual purpose of marriage; it is the actualization of God's plan. This is how it has been. This is how it is.

Yet, our Master says that in the world to come, we are to be neither married, nor given in marriage. (An interesting consideration). We are to be, rather as the angels — spiritual beings who live in an intimate, harmonious community without "the benefit" of marriage.

You probably are aware of the scene in Jesus' life, from which this vision emerges, but if you're not, let me recount it for you. It's the last week of Jesus' life. He's being challenged and set up from all sides, by the religionists of His day. In this scene it's the Sadducees. The rich, liberal religionists who did not believe in the Resurrection and the life beyond. To put him to the test, they tell him a tale of a woman who married seven brothers one-by-one. Each brother died, leaving her by law, obligated to marry the next. So she married them all. They all died. Then she too passed on. "So, whose wife is she going to be in the life to come?" the Sadducees ask, believing of course, there could be no legitimate answer.

"You don't know the Scriptures or the power of God," Jesus replied. "In the life to come they neither marry nor are given in marriage, but are as the angels of God in Heaven" (Matt. 22:22-30).

Now, obviously we are still in the flesh, and we are subject to its limitations and thus we are not equipped for such unbounded spiritual community. Far from it! At our present stage of spiritual development that much intimacy would blow our circuitry! It would be foolish to suppose that in this dimension of life we are prepared to set aside marriage for full, unbounded spiritual intimacy.

We are creatures with a history. Brother Mike and Sister Rose are sharing theirs with you. We are creatures who are called to have integrity with God, ourselves, and others. I see in the lives of Brother Mike and Sister Rose this desire to maintain integrity with each other, with their family, their friends, their employees. And with *you*.

That's one purpose of this book. Another purpose is to bring hope and healing to others. They want their decision to lay aside their roles of husband and wife to each other, to be done with as much integrity as is possible. They continue to care for each other, support and affirm each other as artists and communicators of the Gospel. As ironic as it may seem, they cared for each other enough to let each other go. Gracefully.

Mercifully. (Well, you know, they're still human. All the scenes weren't absolutely elegant).

For Mike and Rose, the roles of husband and wife were causing emotional and spiritual damage. They couldn't be mates for each other for reasons you've probably come to understand in this book. They were unable to fully affirm and nourish each other's personalities as husband and wife. Instead, they evoked each other's "demons": abandonment and you-good-for-nothing shame.

As brother and sister, they are doing quite well with each other. Pray for them. This role transformation is roughly equivalent to a heart transplant. Although, at this point, I am quite optimistic, we are still in a critical-care stage. If you are a part of the true community, continue to pray for their ongoing recovery.

And let us continue in our relationships to be preparing ourselves for the community to come. The intimate community we call Heaven. . . . the ultimate freedom. . . .

It wasn't until after the Renaissance, and its various reformations, that romantic love, as a basis for marriage, was given social sanction. Prior to that time, to violate your marriage vows was to violate your familial community. The teachings of Moses and the Prophets, Jesus, St. Paul, and the apostles on matters of marriage and divorce must be seen in this light. Divorce broke the bonds of the traditional community.

Psychologists tell us there are two primary motivational drives for the human being: the drive toward individualization (becoming a unique person) and autonomy (the ability to make one's own decisions), and the drive toward inclusion and community (being an active, responsible member of society). A person too driven by a desire for inclusion, may become overly dependent and conceptually rigid. Those of us, on the other hand, who are too driven by a desire for uniqueness, run the risk of utterly alienating others by our fierce demands for autonomy. The fact remains, however, that each of us is engaged in a personal quest for individual identity. We want an answer to the questions: "Who am I? Where am I going? What is my purpose?"

The era of the Renaissance roughly demarcates for us the time when our societal values began to shift away from the traditional, tribal value of inclusion, and toward the more personal value of individualization. As with all significant historical change, the shift from the traditional value base to the individual value base was undoubtedly both inevitable and necessary. I don't imagine any of us truly would like to revert to a Middle Ages style of living. The dark ages tormented the soul's desire for autonomy. On the other hand, what we are experiencing today, in the name of freedom and autonomy, is not the epitome of health either! I can quite easily imagine future generations looking back on this era of human history and labeling us as living in the Dark Ages of Intimacy.

Certainly, I do not have an answer for a situation so complex as ours, but my strong belief is that the path to a healthy future lies in the direction of community. This is, of course, in line with the teachings of Jesus and the apostles concerning the age to come. Looking at the traditional, tribal communities of the past, we must, I believe, press forward in establishing various creative forms of intentional community: community by choice, community which both nurtures autonomous exploration and places creative boundaries on inclusion and vice-versa. As John Donne observed, "No man is an island — complete unto himself."

Traditional societies valued the traditional over the individual. We as a society tend to value the individual over the traditional. The intentional community will be created by individuals who are willing to commit themselves to each other's personal development, and to an ongoing process of exploration and negotiation. I have the privilege of experiencing the possible emergence of such community in my work with Mike and Rose and their community of faith and intimacy. (Pray for us).

At the beginning of this century, ninety percent of Americans lived in rural communities. Although personal choice played the deciding role in mate selections, the familial community — parents, grandparents, aunts, uncles, and cousins, the church-and-state — reinforced the institution of marriage. Consequently, at the outset of this century, only one in eighty marriages ended in divorce. Now, what is it? One in four? One in three? One in two? In the Dark Ages of Intimacy, it's as difficult to keep an accurate body count as it must have been in the days of the great plagues.

So what are we to do? We who live in these Dark Ages? Well, we know for certain that God is not *pro-*

divorce. A classic definition of sin is that sin is the breaching of relational bonds. Divorce not only breaks bonds, it most often decimates them!

Yet, neither can we say that God is against divorce in all cases. Thou shalt not divorce is *not* one of the Ten Commandments. Sometimes too much damage has been done, too many trust bonds have been ruptured, to restore a marital relationship.

Hearts and lives are fragile, like glass, and when they are shattered, putting them back together again is a delicate process. The only way forward involves disengaging oneself from a soul-damaging relationship. This does not negate God's power to heal and restore. Rather, it shows how imperfect we are in our humanity. To do this with Christ-like humility, grace and love — now there's the challenge! And thus far, from my viewpoint, Mike and Rose are doing admirably well in their efforts. Continue to support them in your prayers.

I think it's also important, living in times such as ours, to keep in mind the need for us to have a healthy view of God. I think it's important to maintain Jesus' perspective regarding the Father — "the Papa God," Abba, Father. I think it is vitally important to see God as a being who is fundamentally gracious. He is a loving, caring Papa. A Papa who says to His children: "Thou shalt *not* play in the street."

But this is the same Papa who comes running when one of His children lies injured in the street. He doesn't scold, condemn, or berate His child for his or her disobedience. Rather, with tears, He stoops, lifts the child from the pavement, and provides him or her with emergency care.

God is fundamentally a God of mercy, and not primarily a God of law and judgment. He is a Papa, and His laws are for our safety and well-being. And what higher calling is there for us as Christians than to actively reflect God's mercy and love? To reflect it, yes, with compassionate, prophetic proclamation and with the call to obedient living. But even more importantly in these dark and injurious times, we are called to reflect God's mercy in our non-judgmental care of the spiritually wounded.

Remember the story of Jesus, and the woman who was taken in the *act* of adultery? Picture it in your mind. Jesus was at the Temple teaching. The Pharisees — the religious know-it-alls — the shame-and-judgment-mongers — brought a woman up to Him and said, "We took this woman in an act of adultery [Yeah, set her up is more like it!], and we've brought her to you for judgment. Moses says she should be stoned to death. What do you say?"

Jesus said nothing. He just stopped and wrote with His finger in the dirt. God only knows what He wrote. But we can imagine. The same thing which should be written about us each time we pass judgment on one of life's wounded ones! Who are you to judge?

"He that is without sin among you," Jesus said, "let him cast the first stone."

The Lord continued writing, until one-by-one, all the know-it-alls left. The woman stood alone before our Lord.

"Who are your accusers, woman?" Jesus asked with a wry smile. "Does no man condemn you?"

"No man, Lord," she responded. Jesus brushed the dirt from His finger, stood erect and looked the woman straight in the eye, with grace. "Neither do I condemn you. Go. Sin no more."

Now that's mercy, and that's the heart of God.

Thus by grace, a humiliating, life-threatening trauma is transformed. A new beginning is established. Redemption is initiated . . . . .

Rose and Mike have asked me to write a bit about my view of psychotherapy, and how to go about choosing a professional counselor. Well, if you will once again indulge me, let me tell you a story which will, I believe, help you understand more clearly my viewpoint on this matter.

There is a legend that the Great War in Heaven — the initial divorce — began like this. When God created man and woman in His image, He commanded the angels to respect their spiritual sovereignty. Satan, as the legend goes, refused to comply. Satan was God's most loyal angel. He was God's most trusted and beloved angel. Satan refused, on "religious grounds," to comply with God's demand. Satan refused to pay homage to anyone other than God himself. Satan was the first of the religious know-it-alls, and God saw through Satan as quickly, and as surely as He does with all know-it-alls. God saw through the righteous defenses and down to the jealousy. For truly it was so,

Satan was jealous of Adam and Eve: God's new creation. They were the "apple of His eye," so to speak.

So with Satan's act of "religious conscience" and his refusal to reconsider his position, the War in Heaven began. The woman was tempted; the man was seduced. Eden was lost. The division (divorce) between God and people, and between people and people began.

As Isaiah points out, God's ways are not our ways; His thoughts are not our thoughts. The gulf between God and mankind seemed almost unbridgeable.

It was God, of course, who devised the peace plan. (You can read the story for yourself. From Genesis to the Revelation: the story of salvation.) The objective was total reconciliation: complete atonement (at-one-ment). After centuries of careful prophetic preparation. God sent the second Adam, His Son, Jesus, into the world to negotiate the peace. And you know the rest of the story. . . . .

When you are looking for a psychotherapist, what I would recommend is that first you pray to find one who is guided by the Holy Spirit. Look for someone who is actively committed to the plan of at-one-ment. Not someone who is off in an ivory tower telling you the way it "should be." The Master warns us to be especially wary of the "should mongers." They are the Pharisees: the religious know-it-alls. It is they, after all, who crucified our Lord. It was the know-it-alls, and their plans and programs of righteous living and demanding disciplines (guaranteed to produce "demoniac" children) which Jesus consistently confronted and condemned. To the children of the darkness, standing in their rags of light — the demoniac (the psychologically abused and emotionally abandoned; the distressed and maladapted), tax collectors (those who have compromised their ethics and sold their souls to survive in the cut-throat world of busyness) and the prostitutes (those who have despaired of ever being free and pure and whole again), to these the Master says, "Come, Come, be healed. Be at-one again with me. Come."

Likewise, do not choose someone off in the shadows who says, "Well, just do as you please." Look, instead, for someone who knows spiritual reality. One who can help to enable you to discover, claim, unravel and develop your drives for individualization and inclusion, and affirm your journey forward into autonomy and community. Choose one who knows God.

Such a therapist, no matter what his or her theoretical orientation, is going to operate on the assumption that we have at least three levels, domains, aspects, and channels to our being: social, psychological, spiritual.

And the therapist will, in his or her unique fashion, attempt to model him/herself after the Master who embodied these guiding perceptions.

If you are interested in finding a counselor who can serve as a resource for your spiritual quest. I would recommend the following process:

1. Pray. Ask the Lord to guide you. Ask Him to help you determine your wants and needs, and the direction you are to follow.

2. If counseling is the direction in which you perceive you are being led, thank the Lord for His counsel (even if it seems only like a vague intuition at the present time). Ask for His guidance in your selection of a therapist. Listen for His response in your spirit.

3. Be open to the guidance of the Holy Spirit. Consult with those you trust as persons knowledgeable about competent therapists in your area. Continue to pray and be open to the leading of the Holy Spirit as you look and listen.

4. Develop a list of potential therapists.

5. Pray for guidance.

6. Make an appointment for an initial consultation with the therapist of your choice. All you really need is thirty minutes of the therapist's time for this initial visit, unless of course, you are in a crisis. In which case, you may need more than just the one hour usually scheduled. Determine your need, and ascertain the therapist's policy about initial consultations. Many, like myself, only schedule one-hour appointments. Others are able to be more flexible.

   Also, be respectful of the therapist's time and professional status. Don't ask to talk with a therapist by phone for this initial contact, unless you plan to reimburse him/her for the time involved in the purpose of the initial session is for you to ascertain whether or not you and the therapist are compatible. Look. Listen. Be open to your senses, to your intuition, and to the guidance of the Spirit.

7. If the therapist seems appropriate, agree to a few sessions together. With my clients, I consistently ask for a five-session commitment. After five sessions, we can negotiate more. Or we may agree to conclude. In any case, make a commitment and honor it.

8. If you are truly uncertain (not just anxious about the unknown), then take some time. With the Spirit's guidance, scout out a few more possibilities. Make a selection and move forward, or follow the Spirit's guidance along another avenue.

Live your life as your gift to God. In a real sense, God is your only true audience. And on your walk through life, I'll invite you to reflect on something my wife once said to me, "If I want a critic, I'll ask for one. If not, assume that I'm just looking for a cheerleader!" It's a viewpoint worth considering.

Pray for Mike.

Pray for Rose.

Cheer for Mike.

Cheer for Rose...

...and when our journeys and adventures here are done, let's get together at the Party on the other side and swap our stories of life. I'll be looking forward to it!

My Best Friend

I have been by myself for five days. Not totally.
People are everywhere.

I haven't felt alone---even when I have been.

I see people all around me----talking----not too many,
laughing — some only smile----a little —

I am smiling and I'm not with anybody except myself —
am
I finally understanding what it means to be happy within
myself?

I think so!

I like me---I am one of my best friends!

(Rose Hall Warnke)

Afterword

Mike and Rose Hall Warnke are continuing on with their ministries and their lives. They love God and continue to serve Him. This former husband-wife ministry continues to work as friends and as partners in Christ-like grace, humility and love, as a brother and sister in the Lord.

Mike continues, through his God-given gift of humor, to reach people around the world with laughter, hope and Jesus.

Rose continues to reach out to women in prison, she remains involved with her work at Warnke Ministries and is also involved with writing projects and her ministry of music.

Their six children and two grandchildren, ranging ages 2 to 27, are living nearby.

Great is God's faithfulness. Morning by morning new mercies we see.

Counseling Guidelines

by John Joy

If you and your mate are interested in resolving problematic patterns and enhancing your relationship, but you haven't yet managed to "make it happen," here is an approach which might be helpful:

1. Agree together that you are going to see a therapist. Select one and make an appointment. Make it a month or more away. (Like I do with my dentist appointments. Give yourselves plenty of what I call "floss-time").

2. Now that you have your appointment on the books, start your couple "floss-time": the examination, re-negotiating and re-romanticizing of your relationship.
— Go out on a date and talk only of the good times in your relationship. How you met and fell in love. Discuss the favorite scenes of your marriage. Your favorite vacations, holidays, birthdays, anniversaries, and outings. The birth of your children. Favorite places where you've made love, etc.
— Browse in libraries and audio-visual bookstores together, looking for creative approaches in books and tapes that connect with your relationship's needs. Obtain this material and

do the exercises or follow the teachings together.

— Watch favorite movies again together.
— Listen to favorite songs again together. (Particularly songs associated with your courtship, or some positive era of your marriage.)
— Look into marriage-enrichment programs.
— Get in touch with how to give pleasure to each other sensuously. Do body massage with each other letting your mate guide and teach you. Respect his or her wants and wishes.
— Learn to share love, both with and without sex. Communicate about what you like and don't like, gently and with respect.
— Read Ephesians 5:21-33 together, and notice how we are called to submit to one another respectfully in love.

Men:

Love your bride as Christ loves His bride, the Church. Respect and nurture her. Give her every good and perfect gift. Enable her to sense that she is indeed a daughter of the Creator. Just do it, and keep on doing it. . . . .

Women:

Respect and nurture your husband as Mary and Martha did for Christ in the gospels. Believe in him, give him symbols of your admiration. Enable him to sense that he is indeed a son of the Creator! Just do it and keep on doing it . . . . . .

— Attend worship together — regularly.

— Be with good friends together.

— Go on a family retreat.

— Go on another date, and discuss your progress and how to continue to upgrade and fine-tune your relationship. Share your wishes, wants, and needs.

— Respect your mate's requests. Just do it . . . . .

— Go on yet another date and discuss your progress

3. After a few weeks of this sort of dating, evaluate your progress. Do you still believe the appointment with the therapist is necessary? Pray about it. Talk about it. If it's your sense that your marriage is back on track and "clicking" again, cancel your appointment.

4. If, however, in a few weeks time, you have not been able to satisfactorily get your relationship back on track, if there are still unresolved issues and conflicts which continue to hamper your ability to be intimately supportive of one

another, then keep your previously scheduled appointment, and move forward.

5. May the Grace of Christ guide you, and may you allow His spirit to ever direct your quest for personal identity and spiritual integrity. May God be with you. May you ever listen to His voice resonating in your deep self. Live your life before His eyes with honor, grace, style, and creative zeal.